Machine Learning Projects for Mobile Applications

Build Android and iOS applications using TensorFlow Lite and Core ML

Karthikeyan NG

BIRMINGHAM - MUMBAI

Machine Learning Projects for Mobile Applications

Commissioning Editor: Sunith Shetty
Acquisition Editor: Dayne Castelino
Content Development Editor: Rhea Henriques
Technical Editor: Sayli Nikalje
Copy Editor: Safis Editing
Project Coordinator: Manthan Patel
Proofreader: Safis Editing
Indexer: Mariammal Chettiyar
Graphics: Jisha Chirayil
Production Coordinator: Aparna Bhagat

First published: October 2018

Production reference: 1311018

Published by Packt Publishing Ltd.
Livery Place
35 Livery Street
Birmingham
B3 2PB, UK.

ISBN 978-1-78899-459-0

www.packtpub.com

To my wife, Nanthana, for putting up with me during the course of this book. I know it must not have been easy.

To my parents, for their constant support.

`mapt.io`

Mapt is an online digital library that gives you full access to over 5,000 books and videos, as well as industry leading tools to help you plan your personal development and advance your career. For more information, please visit our website.

Why subscribe?

- Spend less time learning and more time coding with practical eBooks and Videos from over 4,000 industry professionals

- Improve your learning with Skill Plans built especially for you

- Get a free eBook or video every month

- Mapt is fully searchable

- Copy and paste, print, and bookmark content

Packt.com

Did you know that Packt offers eBook versions of every book published, with PDF and ePub files available? You can upgrade to the eBook version at `www.packt.com` and as a print book customer, you are entitled to a discount on the eBook copy. Get in touch with us at `customercare@packtpub.com` for more details.

At `www.packt.com`, you can also read a collection of free technical articles, sign up for a range of free newsletters, and receive exclusive discounts and offers on Packt books and eBooks.

Contributors

About the author

Karthikeyan NG is the Head of Engineering and Technology at the Indian lifestyle and fashion retail brand. He served as a software engineer at Symantec Corporation and has worked with two US-based startups as an early employee and has built various products. He has 9+ years of experience in various scalable products using Web, Mobile, ML, AR, and VR technologies. He is an aspiring entrepreneur and technology evangelist. His interests lie in exploring new technologies and innovative ideas to resolve a problem. He has also bagged prizes from more than 15 hackathons, is a TEDx speaker and a speaker at technology conferences and meetups as well as guest lecturer at a Bengaluru University. When not at work, he is found trekking.

I would like to thank Saurav Satpathy for helping me with the codes in one of the chapters. I would like to extend my gratitude to Varsha Shetty for presenting the idea of the book, and to Rhea Henriques for her tenacity. Thanks to Akshi, Tejas, Sayli, and the technical reviewer, Mayur, and the editorial team. I would also like to thank the open source community for making this book possible with the frameworks on both Android and iOS platforms.

About the reviewer

Mayur Ravindra Narkhede has a good blend of experience in data science and industrial domain. He is a researcher with a B.Tech in computer science and an M.Tech in CSE with a specialization in Artificial Intelligence.

A data scientist whose core experience lies in building automated end-to-end solutions, he is proficient at applying technology, AI, ML, data mining, and design thinking to better understand and predict improvements in business functions and desirable requirements with growth profitability.

He has worked on multiple advanced solutions, such as ML and predictive model development for the oil and gas industry, financial services, road traffic and transport, life sciences, and the big data platform for asset-intensive industries.

Packt is searching for authors like you

If you're interested in becoming an author for Packt, please visit `authors.packtpub.com` and apply today. We have worked with thousands of developers and tech professionals, just like you, to help them share their insight with the global tech community. You can make a general application, apply for a specific hot topic that we are recruiting an author for, or submit your own idea.

Table of Contents

Preface

Machine learning is a growing technique that focuses on the development of computer programs that can be changed or modified when exposed to new data. It has made significant advances that have enabled practical applications of **machine learning** (**ML**) and, by extension, the overall field of **Artificial Intelligence** (**AI**).

This book presents the implementation of seven practical, real-world projects that will teach you how to leverage TensorFlow Lite and Core ML to perform efficient machine learning. We will be learning about the recent advancements in TensorFlow and its extensions, such as TensorFlow Lite, to design intelligent apps that learn from complex/large datasets. We will delve into advancements such as deep learning by building apps using deep neural network architecture such as **Convolutional Neural Networks** (**CNNs**), **recurrent neural networks** (**RNNs**), transfer learning, and much more.

By the end of this book, you will not only have mastered all the concepts of and learned how to implement machine learning and deep learning, but you will also have learned how to solve the problems and challenges faced while building powerful apps on mobile using TensorFlow Lite and Core ML.

Who this book is for

Machine Learning Projects for Mobile Applications is for you if you are a data scientist, ML expert, deep learning, or AI enthusiast who fancies mastering ML and deep learning implementation with practical examples using TensorFlow and Keras. Basic knowledge of Python programming language would be an added advantage.

What this book covers

Chapter 1, *Mobile Landscapes in Machine Learning,* makes us familiar with the basic ideas behind TensorFlow Lite and Core ML.

Chapter 2, *CNN Based Age and Gender Identification Using Core ML,* teaches us how to build an iOS application to detect the age, gender, and emotion of a person from a camera feed or from the user's photo gallery using the existing data models that were built for the same purpose.

Chapter 3, *Applying Neural Style Transfer on Photos*, teaches us how to build a complete iOS and Android application in which image transformations are applied to our own images in a fashion similar to the Instagram app.

Chapter 4, *Deep Diving into the ML Kit with Firebase*, explores the Google Firebase-based ML Kit platform for mobile applications.

Chapter 5, *A Snapchat-Like AR Filter on Android*, takes us on a journey where we will build an AR filter that is used on applications such as Snapchat and Instagram using TensorFlow Lite.

Chapter 6, *Handwritten Digit Classifier Using Adversarial Learning*, explains how to build an Android application that identifies handwritten digits.

Chapter 7, *Face-Swapping with Your Friends Using OpenCV*, takes a close look at building an application where a face in an image is replaced by another face.

Chapter 8, *Classifying Food Using Transfer Learning*, explains how to classify food items using transfer learning.

Chapter 9, *What's Next?*, gives us a glimpse into all the applications built throughout the book and their relevance in the future.

To get the most out of this book

If you have prior knowledge of building mobile apps, that will help greatly. If not, it is advisable to learn the basics of Java or Kotlin for Android, or Swift for iOS.

If you have basic knowledge of Python, that will help you build your own data model, but Python skill is not mandatory.

The applications in the book are built using a MacBook Pro. Most of the command-line operations are shown with the assumption that you have a bash shell installed on your machine. They may not work in a Windows development environment.

Download the code

You can download the example code files for this book from your account at www.packt.com. If you purchased this book elsewhere, you can visit www.packt.com/support and register to have the files emailed directly to you.

You can download the code files by following these steps:

1. Log in or register at www.packt.com.
2. Select the **SUPPORT** tab.
3. Click on **Code Downloads & Errata**.
4. Enter the name of the book in the **Search** box and follow the onscreen instructions.

Once the file is downloaded, please make sure that you unzip or extract the folder using the latest version of:

- WinRAR/7-Zip for Windows
- Zipeg/iZip/UnRarX for Mac
- 7-Zip/PeaZip for Linux

The code bundle for the book is also hosted on GitHub at https://github.com/ PacktPublishing/Machine-Learning-Projects-for-Mobile-Applications. In case there's an update to the code, it will be updated on the existing GitHub repository.

We also have other code bundles from our rich catalog of books and videos available at https://github.com/PacktPublishing/. Check them out!

Download the color images

We also provide a PDF file that has color images of the screenshots/diagrams used in this book. You can download it here: https://www.packtpub.com/sites/default/files/ downloads/9781788994590_ColorImages.pdf.

Conventions used

There are a number of text conventions used throughout this book.

CodeInText: Indicates code words in text, database table names, folder names, filenames, file extensions, pathnames, dummy URLs, user input, and Twitter handles. Here is an example: "So, we will start our iterations from 1.0 and start minimizing errors in the right direction."

A block of code is set as follows:

```
def estimate_house_price(sqft, location):
 price = < DO MAGIC HERE >
 return price
```

Any command-line input or output is written as follows:

```
/usr/bin/ruby -e "$(curl -fsSL \
    https://raw.githubusercontent.com/Homebrew/install/master/install)"
```

Bold: Indicates a new term, an important word, or words that you see onscreen. For example, words in menus or dialog boxes appear in the text like this. Here is an example: "Let's select **Single View App** from the initial screen, illustrated in this screenshot."

 Warnings or important notes appear like this.

 Tips and tricks appear like this.

Get in touch

Feedback from our readers is always welcome.

General feedback: If you have questions about any aspect of this book, mention the book title in the subject of your message and email us at customercare@packtpub.com.

Errata: Although we have taken every care to ensure the accuracy of our content, mistakes do happen. If you have found a mistake in this book, we would be grateful if you would report this to us. Please visit www.packt.com/submit-errata, selecting your book, clicking on the Errata Submission Form link, and entering the details.

Piracy: If you come across any illegal copies of our works in any form on the Internet, we would be grateful if you would provide us with the location address or website name. Please contact us at copyright@packt.com with a link to the material.

If you are interested in becoming an author: If there is a topic that you have expertise in and you are interested in either writing or contributing to a book, please visit authors.packtpub.com.

Reviews

Please leave a review. Once you have read and used this book, why not leave a review on the site that you purchased it from? Potential readers can then see and use your unbiased opinion to make purchase decisions, we at Packt can understand what you think about our products, and our authors can see your feedback on their book. Thank you!

For more information about Packt, please visit `packt.com`.

Mobile Landscapes in Machine Learning

Computers are improving by the day, and device form factors are changing tremendously. In the past, we would only see computers at offices, but now we see them on our home desks, on our laps, in our pockets, and on our wrists. The market is becoming increasingly varied as machines are being equipped with more and more intelligence.

Almost every adult currently carries a device around with them, and it is estimated that we look at our smartphones at least 50 times a day, whether there is a need to or not. These machines affect our daily decision-making processes. Devices are now equipped with applications such as Siri, Google Assistant, Alexa, or Cortana, features that are designed to mimic human intelligence. The ability to answer any query thrown at them presents these types of technology as *master humans*. On the backend, these systems improve using the collective intelligence acquired from all users. The more you interact with virtual assistants, the better are the results they give out.

Despite these advancements, how much closer are we to creating a human brain through a machine? We are in 2018 now. If science discovers a way to control the neurons of our brain, this may be possible in the near future. Machines that mimic the capabilities of a human are helping to solve complex textual, visual, and audio problems. They resemble the tasks carried out by a human brain on a daily basis—on average, the human brain makes approximately 35,000 decisions in a day.

While we will be able to mimic the human brain in the future, it will come at a cost. We don't have a cheaper solution for it at the moment. The magnitude of power consumption of a human brain simulation program limits it in comparison to a human brain. The human brain consumes about 20 W of power, while a simulation program consumes about 1 MW of power or more. Neurons in the human brain operate at a speed of 200 Hz, while a typical microprocessor operates at a speed of 2 GHz, which is 10 million times more than that.

While we are still far from cloning a human brain, we can implement an algorithm that makes conscious decisions based on previous data as well as data from similar devices. This is where the subset of **Artificial Intelligence** (**AI**) comes in handy. With predefined algorithms that identify patterns from the complex data we have, these types of intelligence can then give us useful information.

When the computer starts making decisions without being instructed explicitly every time, we achieve **machine learning** (**ML**) capability. ML is used everywhere right now, including through features such as identifying email spam, recommending the best product to buy on an e-commerce website, tagging your face automatically on a social media photograph, and so on. All of these are done using the patterns identified in historical data, and also through algorithms that reduce unnecessary noise from the data and produce quality output. When the data accumulates more and more, the computers can make better decisions.

Since we have wider access to mobile devices and the amount of time we spend on those devices is rapidly increasing, it makes sense to run ML models on the mobile phone itself. In the mobile phone market, Android and iOS platforms take the lead to cover the whole smartphone spectrum. We will explore how TensorFlow Lite and Core ML works on these mobile platforms.

The topics that will be covered in this chapter are as follows:

- ML basics (with an example)
- TensorFlow and Core ML basics

Machine learning basics

ML is a concept that describes the process of a set of generic algorithms analyzing your data, and providing you with interesting data without writing any specific codes for your problem.

Alternatively, we can look at ML as a black box how cutting edge scientists are using it to do something crazy like detecting epilepsy or cancer disease, yet your simple email inbox is using it to filter spam every day.

On a larger level, ML can be classified into the following two categories:

- Supervised learning
- Unsupervised learning

Supervised learning

With supervised learning, your main task is to develop a function that maps inputs to outputs. For example, if you have input variables (x) and an output variable (y), then you can use an algorithm to learn the mapping function from the input to the output:

$$y = f(x)$$

The goal is to approximate the mapping function so well that when you have new input data (x), you can predict the output variables (y) for it.

For example, you have a bunch of fruits and baskets. You have started labeling the fruits and baskets as apple, banana, strawberry, etc., When you are done with labeling all the fruits into their corresponding baskets, now your job is to label the new fruit that comes in. You have already learnt all the fruits and their details by labeling them. Based on the previous experience you can now label the new fruit based on its attributes like color, size and pattern.

Unsupervised learning

In this case, you only have input data (x) and no corresponding output variables. The goal for unsupervised learning is to model the underlying structure or distribution in the data in order to learn more about it.

In unsupervised learning, you may not have any data in the beginning. Say for example on the same scenario discussed above in supervised learning, you have a basket full of fruits and you are asked to group them into similar groups. But you don't have any previous data or there are no training or labeling is done earlier. In that case, you need to understand the domain first because you have no idea whether the input is a fruit or not. In that case, you need to first understand all the characteristics of every input and then to try to match with every new input. May be at the final step you might have classified all the red color fruits into one baskets and the green color fruits into another basket. But not an accurate classification. This is called as unsupervised learning.

Linear regression - supervised learning

Let's look at one simple example of linear regression with its implementation on TensorFlow.

Let's predict the price of a house, looking at the prices of other houses in the same area along with its size information:

$82000 $55500   ???

We have a house that costs $82,000 and another one at $55,000. Now, our task is to find the price of the third house. We know the sizes of all of the houses along with the prices, and we can map this data in a graph. Let's find out the price of the third house based on the other two data points that we have:

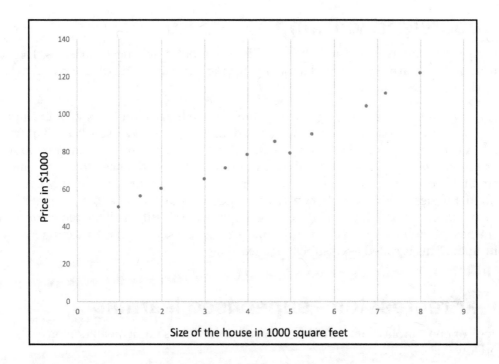

You may wonder how to draw the line now. Draw a random line close to all the points marked on the graph. Now, calculate the distance from each point to the line and add them together. The result of this is the error value. Our algorithm should move toward minimizing the error, because the best fit line has a lower error value. This procedure is known as a **gradient descent**.

The prices of all the houses in the particular locality are mapped on the graph accordingly. Now, let's plot the values of the two houses that we already know:

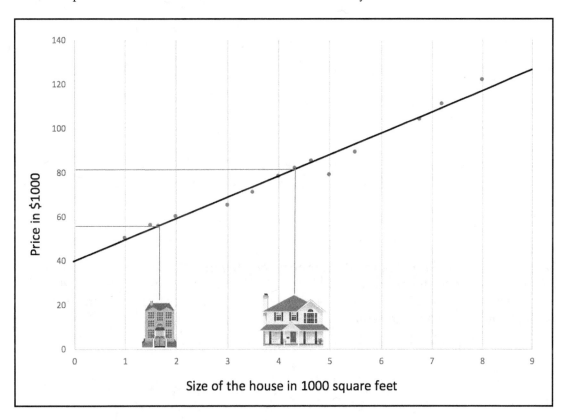

After that, let's draw one line that passes closer to most of the values. The line fits the data perfectly. From this, we should be able to identify the price of house number three:

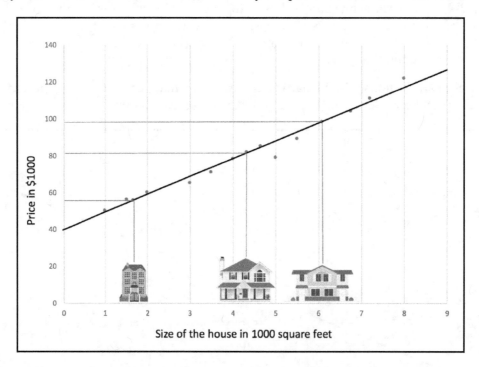

Based on the size of the data provided for home number three, we can map the size of the data provided for the home number on the graph. This will allow us to figure out the connecting point on the line drawn through all points. That maps to $98,300 on the *y* axis. This is known as **linear regression**:

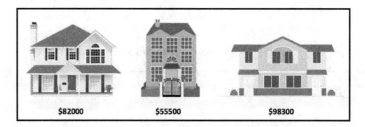

Let's try to translate our problem into the form of a pseudocode:

```
def estimate_house_price(sqft, location):
 price = 0
 #In my area, the average house costs 2000 per sq.ft
 price_per_sqft = 2000
 if location == "vegas":
     #but some areas cost a bit more
     price_per_sqft = 5000
 elif location == "newyork":
     #and some areas cost less
     price_per_sqft = 4000
 #start with a base price estimate based on how big the place is
 price = price_per_sqft * sqft
 return price
```

This will be your typical method for estimating the house price. We can keep adding more and more condition checks to this, but it can't be controlled beyond the point at which the number of locations or the parameter increases. For a typical house price estimation, there are a lot of other factors also considered, such as the number of rooms, locations in the vicinity, schools, gas stations, hospitals, water level, transport, and so on. We can generalize this function into something very simple and guess the right answer:

```
def estimate_house_price(sqft, location):
 price = < DO MAGIC HERE >
 return price
```

How can we identify a line that fits perfectly without writing condition checks? Typically, the linear regression line is represented in the following form:

$$Y = XW + b$$

In our example, let's put this into a more simple form in order to gain a better understanding:

$$prediction = X * Weight + bias$$

Weight is the slope of the line and *bias* is the intercept (the value of *Y* when *X* = 0). After constructing the linear model, we need to identify the gradient descent. The *cost* function identifies the mean squared error to bring out the gradient descent:

$$cost = \sum_{i=1}^{50} \frac{(randomguess(i) - realanswer(i))^2}{50 * 2}$$

Let's represent the *cost* function through pseudocode to solve our problem of estimating the house price:

```
def estimate_house_price(sqft, location):
 price = 0
 #and this
 price += sqft * 235.43
 #maybe this too
 price += location * 643.34
 #adding a little bit of salt for a perfect result
 price += 191.23
 return price
```

The values 235.43, 643.34, and 191.23 may look random, but with these values we are able to discover the estimation of any new house. How do we arrive at this value? We should do an iteration to arrive at the right value while reducing our error in the right direction:

```
def estimate_house_price(sqft, location):
 price = 0
 #and this
 price += sqft * 1.0
 #maybe this too
 price += location * 1.0
 #adding a little bit of salt for a perfect result
 price += 1.0
 return price
```

So, we will start our iterations from 1.0 and start minimizing errors in the right direction. Let's put this into code using TensorFlow. We will look at the methods that are used in more depth later on:

```
#import all the necessary libraries
import tensorflow as tf
import matplotlib.pyplot as plt
import numpy

#Random number generator
randnumgen = numpy.random

#The values that we have plotted on the graph
values_X =
  numpy.asarray([1,2,3,4,5.5,6.75,7.2,8,3.5,4.65,5,1.5,4.32,1.65,6.08])
values_Y =
  numpy.asarray([50,60,65,78,89,104,111,122,71,85,79,56,81.8,55.5,98.3])

# Parameters
```

```
learning_rate = 0.01
training_steps = 1000
iterations = values_X.shape[0]

# tf float points - graph inputs
X = tf.placeholder("float")
Y = tf.placeholder("float")

# Set the weight and bias
W = tf.Variable(randnumgen.randn(), name="weight")
b = tf.Variable(randnumgen.randn(), name="bias")

# Linear model construction
# y = xw + b
prediction = tf.add(tf.multiply(X, W), b)

#The cost method helps to minimize error for gradient descent.
#This is called mean squared error.
cost = tf.reduce_sum(tf.pow(prediction-Y, 2))/(2*iterations)

# In TensorFlow, minimize() method knows how to optimize the values for #
weight & bias.
optimizer =
    tf.train.GradientDescentOptimizer(learning_rate).minimize(cost)

#assigning default values
init = tf.global_variables_initializer()

#We can start the training now
with tf.Session() as sess:

    # Run the initializer. We will see more in detail with later
    #chapters
     sess.run(init)

    # Fit all training data
     for step in range(training_steps):
         for (x, y) in zip(values_X, values_Y):
             sess.run(optimizer, feed_dict={X: x, Y: y})
             c = sess.run(cost, feed_dict={X: values_X, Y:values_Y})
             print("Step:", '%04d' % (step+1), "cost=", "
                         {:.4f}".format(c), \
                         "W=", sess.run(W), "b=", sess.run(b))

    print("Successfully completed!")
    # with this we can identify the values of Weight & bias
    training_cost = sess.run(cost, feed_dict={X: values_X, Y:
                                            values_Y})
```

```
print("Training cost=", training_cost, "Weight=", sess.run(W),
        "bias=", sess.run(b))

# Lets plot all the values on the graph
plt.plot(values_X, values_Y, 'ro', label='house price points')
plt.plot(values_X, sess.run(W) * values_X + sess.run(b),
                                  label='Line Fitting')
plt.legend()
plt.show()
```

You can find the same code from our GitHub repository (`https://github.com/PacktPublishing/Machine-Learning-Projects-for-Mobile-Applications`) under Chapter01.

TensorFlow Lite and Core ML

A good starting point for this book would be to get our hands dirty playing with the ML model dataset and training the model. It will be useful to jump in quickly in further chapters. We are not going to deal with basic ML algorithms here; instead, this will be more of a practical-based approach. You can download the complete code base from our GitHub repository (`https://github.com/intrepidkarthi/MLmobileapps`).

Throughout this book, we will deal with two frameworks: TensorFlow Lite and Core ML. These two frameworks are tightly coupled with Android and iOS. We will look into the basics of ML on a mobile device with TensorFlow Lite. It is assumed that the reader knows the basics of TensorFlow and basic ML algorithms, because this book is not going to cover those elements.

As previously stated, every one of us is holding a smartphone in our pocket almost all of the time. We have a rich amount of data that comes from the sensors available on these devices. As well as this, we have data that is coming from edge devices. At the time of writing this book, there are close to 23 billion devices under this category, including smart speakers, smart watches, and smart sensors. High-end technologies that used to only be available on costlier devices are now available on cheaper devices as well. This exponential rate of growth for these devices paves the way to ML on these devices.

While there are many reasons to run ML on the devices, the foremost reason is that of latency. If you are processing video or audio, you don't want to keep pinging the server with data to and fro. Another advantage is that you can do the processing when the device is in offline mode. Importantly, the data stays on the device itself, local to the user. This is more energy-efficient in terms of battery/power consumption.

While this looks like an advantage, there are also a few cons to this approach. Most of our devices are running on batteries with limited capacity, less processing capability, and strict memory constraints. The TensorFlow framework won't resolve all these issues, which is why it has shifted to have a framework that works efficiently under all these conditions. TensorFlow Lite is a lightweight, energy-and memory-efficient framework that will run on embedded smaller-form factor devices.

TensorFlow Lite

The TensorFlow Lite framework consists of five high-level components. All of these components are optimized to run on a mobile platform as shown below in the architecture diagram:

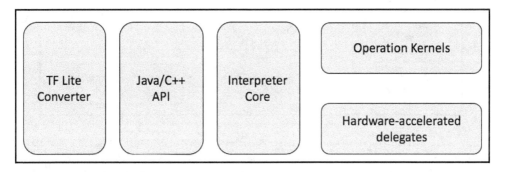

Here are the core units of the TensorFlow Lite architecture:

- The first part is to convert your existing model into a TensorFlow Lite-compatible model (.tflite) using the TensorFlow Lite Converter, and have your trained model on the disk itself. You can also use the pre-trained model in your mobile or embedded applications.
- Java/C++ API—the API loads the .tflite model and invokes the interpreter. It is available on all platforms. Java API is a wrapper written on top of C++ API, and it is available only on Android.
- Interpreter and kernels—the interpreter module operates with the help of operation kernels. It loads kernels selectively; the size of the core interpreter is 75 KB. This is a significant reduction on TensorFlow Lite from the 1.1 MB required by TensorFlow Mobile. With all the supported ops, its core interpreter size comes to 400 KB. Developers can selectively choose which ops they want to include. In that way, they can keep the footprint small.

- H/W accelerated delegates—on select Android devices, the interpreter will use the Android **Neural Networks API** (**NNAPI**) for hardware acceleration, or default to CPU execution if none are available.

You can also implement custom kernels using the C++ API that can be used by the interpreter.

Supported platforms

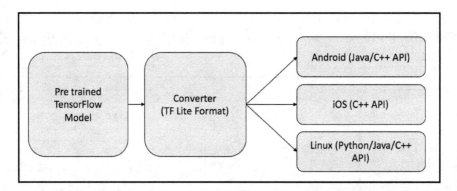

TensorFlow Lite currently supports Android/iOS platforms as well as Linux (for example Raspberry Pi) platforms. On embedded devices such as Raspberry Pi, Python API helps. TensorFlow Lite platforms also support Core ML models as well as iOS platforms.

On iOS platforms, from the pre-trained TensorFlow model, we can directly convert the format into the Core ML model where the app will directly run on the Core ML runtime:

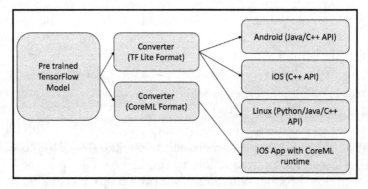

With a single model, we can run the model on both Android/iOS platforms by converting the formats.

TensorFlow Lite memory usage and performance

TensorFlow uses FlatBuffers for the model. FlatBuffers is a cross-platform, open source serialization library. The main advantage of using FlatBuffers is that it does not need a secondary representation before accessing the data through packing/unpacking. It is often coupled with per-object memory allocation. FlatBuffers is more memory-efficient than Protocol Buffers because it helps us to keep the memory footprint small.

FlatBuffers was originally developed for gaming platforms. It is also used in other platforms since it is performance-sensitive. At the time of conversion, TensorFlow Lite pre-fuses the activations and biases, allowing TensorFlow Lite to execute faster. The interpreter uses static memory and execution plans that allow it to load faster. The optimized operation kernels run faster on the NEON and ARM platforms.

TensorFlow takes advantage of all innovations that happen on a silicon level on these devices. TensorFlow Lite supports the Android NNAPI. At the time of writing, a few of the **Oracle Enterprise Managers** (**OEMs**) have started using the NNAPI. TensorFlow Lite uses direct graphics acceleration, which uses **Open Graphics Library** (**OpenGL**) on Android and Metal on iOS.

To improve performance, there have been changes to quantization. This is a technique to store numbers and perform calculations on them. This helps in two ways. Firstly, as long as the model is smaller, it is better for smaller devices. Secondly, many processors have specialized synthe instruction sets, which process fixed-point operands much faster than they process floating point numbers. So, a very naive way to do quantization would be to simply shrink the weights and activations after you are done training. However, this leads to suboptimal accuracies.

TensorFlow Lite gives three times the performance of TensorFlow on MobileNet and Inception-v3. While TensorFlow Lite only supports inference, it will soon be adapted to also have a training module in it. TensorFlow Lite supports around 50 commonly used operations.

It supports MobileNet, Inception-v3, ResNet50, SqueezeNet, DenseNet, Inception-v4, SmartReply, and others:

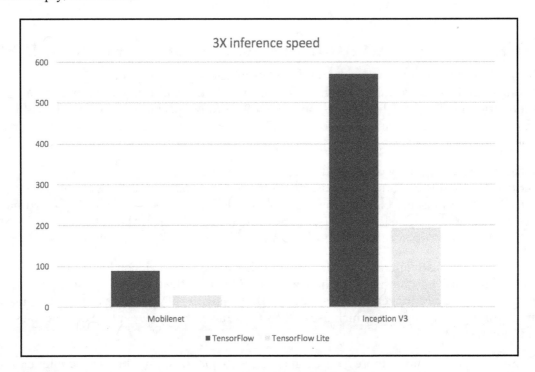

 The *y* axis in the graph is measured in milliseconds.

Hands-on with TensorFlow Lite

With TensorFlow Lite, you can use an existing model to quickly start building your first TensorFlow Lite-based application:

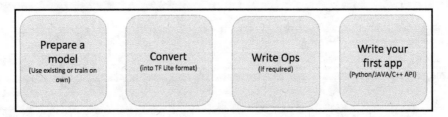

Using TensorFlow Lite in real time consists of four steps:

1. In the first step, we need to either use an existing model or prepare our own model and train it.
2. Once the model is ready, it needs to be converted into .tflite format using converters.
3. Then, we can write ops on top of it for any kind of optimization.
4. You can start writing your hello world project.

Let's jump straight into the code from here.

Converting SavedModel into TensorFlow Lite format

Converting your ML model into a TensorFlow Lite model can be done in just one line of code by calling the conversion method. Here is the simple Python snippet that converts your existing model into TensorFlow Lite format. You can feed in the existing model and convert that into .tflite format:

```
import sys
from tf.contrib.lite import convert_savedmodel
convert_savedmodel.convert(
                    saved_model_directory="/tmp/your_model",
                    output_tflite_file="/tmp/my_model.tflite")
```

The code here converts the existing model created in other frameworks into TensorFlow Lite format using FlatBuffers. There are a few conversion strategies that need to be followed.

Strategies

We implement the following strategies:

- Use a frozen graphdef (or SavedModel)
- Avoid unsupported operators

- Use visualizers to understand the model (TensorBoard and TensorFlow Lite visualizer)
- Write custom operators for any missing functionality
- If anything is missed out, file an issue with the community

We will see these strategies in detail when we go further into practical applications in future chapters.

TensorFlow Lite on Android

We can start using the demo app provided in the TensorFlow GitHub repository. This is a camera application that classifies images continuously using either a floating point Inception-v3 model or a quantized MobileNet model. Try this using Android Version 5.0 or preceding.

 The demo app can be found at: `https://github.com/tensorflow/`
`tensorflow/tree/master/tensorflow/contrib/lite/java/demo/app`.

This application performs real-time classification of frames. It displays the top most-probable classification categories. It also displays the time taken to detect the object.

There are three ways to get the demo app on your device:

- You can download the APK binary, which is pre-built
- You can build on Android Studio and run the application
- You can use Bazel to download the source code of TensorFlow Lite, and run the app through the command line

Downloading the APK binary

This is the easiest way to try the application.

Once you install the app, start the application. When you open the app for the first time, it will prompt you to access the device camera using runtime permissions. Once the permissions are enabled, you can use the app to recognize objects in the real-time back camera view. In the results, you can see the top three classifications for the identified object, along with the latency.

TensorFlow Lite on Android Studio

You can download and build TensorFlow Lite directly from Android Studio
by following these steps:

1. Download and install the latest version of Android Studio.
2. In your studio settings, make sure that the NDK version is greater than 14 and the SDK version is greater than 26. We are using 27 in this book and on further applications. We will look in detail at how to configure this in further projects.
3. You can download the application from the link in the following information box.
4. As Android Studio instructs, you need to install all the Gradle dependencies.

 The demo app can be found at: `https://github.com/tensorflow/tensorflow/tree/master/tensorflow/contrib/lite/java/demo/app/src/main/java/com/example/android/tflitecamerademo`.

We need a model in order to use it in the application. We can either use an existing model or train our own model. Let's use an existing model in this application.

You can download models at the link given next, in the information box. You can also download the zipped model file from the link given:

- You can download an Inception-v3 floating point model or the latest MobileNet model. Copy the appropriate `.tflite` to the Android app's `assets` directory. You can then change the classifier in the `Camera2BasicFragment.java` file, `tensorflow/contrib/lite/java/demo/app/src/main/assets/`.

 The models can be downloaded from: `https://github.com/tensorflow/tensorflow/blob/master/tensorflow/contrib/lite/g3doc/models.md`.

Now, you can build and run the demo app.

Building the TensorFlow Lite demo app from the source

As a first step, clone the TensorFlow repo. You need Bazel to build the APK:

```
git clone https://github.com/tensorflow/tensorflow
```

Installing Bazel

If Bazel is not installed on your system, you need to install it. This book is written according to the macOS High Sierra 10.13.2 experience. Bazel is installed through Homebrew.

Installing using Homebrew

The following are the steps to install Homebrew:

1. Homebrew has dependency with JDK, which you need to install first. Download the latest JDK from the Oracle website and install it.
2. Then, install Homebrew.

You can run the following script directly from Terminal:

```
/usr/bin/ruby -e "$(curl -fsSL \
    https://raw.githubusercontent.com/Homebrew/install/master/install)"
```

Once Homebrew is installed, you can install Bazel with the following command:

```
brew install bazel
```

All is well. Now, you can verify the Bazel version using the command shown here:

```
bazel version
```

If Bazel is already installed, you can upgrade the version using this command:

```
brew upgrade bazel
```

Note that Bazel does not currently support Android builds on Windows. Windows users should download the pre-built binary.

Installing Android NDK and SDK

You need Android NDK to build the TensorFlow Lite code. You can download this from NDK Archives, accessed through the following link.

Android NDK Archives can be downloaded from: `https://developer.android.com/ndk/downloads/older_releases`.

Android Studio comes with SDK tools. You need to access build tools version 23 or higher (the application runs on devices with API 21 or higher).

You can update the WORKSPACE file in the root of the directory with the API level and path to both SDK and NDK.

Update the api_level and location of the SDK and NDK at the root of the repository. If you open SDK Manager from Studio, you can find the SDK path. For example, note the following for SDK:

```
android_sdk_repository (
  name = "androidsdk",
  api_level = 27,
  build_tools_version = "27.0.3",
  path = "/Users/coco/Library/Android/sdk",
)
```

And for Android NDK archives:

```
android_ndk_repository(
  name = "androidndk",
  path = "/home/coco/android-ndk-r14b/",
  api_level = 19,
)
```

At the time of writing, android-ndk-r14b-darwin-x86_64.zip is used from the NDK Archives. You can adjust the preceding parameters based on the availability.

Now, we are ready to build the source code. To build the demo app, run Bazel:

```
bazel build --cxxopt=--std=c++11
  //tensorflow/contrib/lite/java/demo/app/src/main:TfLiteCameraDemo
```

Caution: Due to a bug, Bazel only supports the Python 2 environment right now.

MobileNet is a good place to start ML. The model images from this dataset consist of images in 299 * 299 pixel. But, the camera captures in a 224 * 224 pixel image and resizes it to match the size in the model. It occupies 224 * 224 * 3 bytes in the disk, per image. These bytes are converted into ByteBuffer row by row after that. Here, the number 3 represents RGB values of a pixel.

The demo app here uses the TensorFlow Lite Java API, which takes a single image as input and produces the same in output. The output contains a two-dimensional array. The first array contains the category index value, and the second dimension contains the confidence value of the classification. From the values, it displays the top three to the user on the frontend.

TensorFlow Lite on iOS

Now, we will build the same application on the iOS environment. The app has the same features, and we will also use the same quantized MobileNet model. We need to run it on a real iOS device to use the camera functionality; it won't work on a simulator.

Prerequisites

To begin using Xcode, you need to have a valid Apple developer ID on their portal. This application also requires an iPhone since it uses the camera module. You need to have the provisioning profile assigned to the particular device. Only then should you be able to build and run the application on the device.

You can clone the complete TensorFlow repository, but to run this application you may not need the complete source code. If you have downloaded it already, you don't need to do it again:

```
git clone https://github.com/tensorflow/tensorflow
```

Xcode comes with command-line tools, as shown here:

```
xcode-select --install
```

Building the iOS demo app

If you are not very familiar with iOS application building, please look at some basic tutorials for this. You need to install cocoapods to install all the dependencies:

```
sudo gem install cocoapods
```

There is a shell script available to download the model files required to run this application:

```
sh tensorflow/contrib/lite/examples/ios/download_models.sh
```

You can go to the project directory and install `pod` from the command line:

```
cd tensorflow/contrib/lite/examples/ios/camera
pod install
pod update
```

Once the update is done, you should be able to see
`tflite_camera_example.xcworkspace`. Then, you can open the application in Xcode.
You can use the following command as well:

```
open tflite_camera_example.xcworkspace
```

It is now time to build and run the application on your iPhone.

You need to allow the app the user permissions for camera usage. Use the camera to point
to objects, and start seeing the classification results!

Core ML

Core ML helps us to build ML learning applications for iOS platforms.

Core ML uses trained models that make predictions based on new input data. For example,
a model that's been trained on a region's historical land prices may be able to predict the
price of land when given the details of locality and size.

Core ML acts as a foundation for other frameworks that are domain-specific. The major
frameworks that Core ML supports include GamePlayKit to evaluate the learned decision
trees, **natural language processing (NLP)** for text analysis, and vision framework for
image-based analysis.

Core ML is built on top of accelerate, **basic neural network subroutines (BNNSs)**, and
Metal Performance Shaders, as shown in the architecture diagram from the Core ML
documentation:

- With the Accelerate Framework, you can do mathematical computations on a
  large scale as well as calculations based on images. It is optimized for high
  performance and also contains APIs written in C for vector and matrix
  calculations, **Digital Signal Processing (DSP)**, and other computations.
- BNNS help to implement neural networks. From the training data, the
  subroutine methods and other collections are useful for implementing and
  running neural network.

- With the Metal framework, you can render advanced three-dimensional graphics and run parallel computations using the GPU device. It comes with Metal shading language, the MetalKit framework, and the Metal Performance Shaders framework. With the Metal Performance Shaders framework, it is tuned to work with the hardware features of each GPU family for optimal performance.

Core ML applications are built on top of the three layers of components mentioned, as shown in the following diagram:

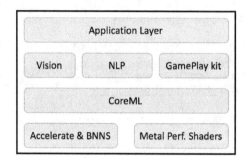

Core ML is optimized for on-device performance, which minimizes memory footprint and power consumption.

Core ML model conversion

To run your first application on iOS, you don't need to start building your own model. You can use any one of the best existing models. If you have a model that is created using another third-party framework, you can use the Core ML Tools Python package, or third-party packages such as MXNet converter or TensorFlow converter. The links to access these tools are given next. If your model doesn't support any of these converters, you can also write your own converter.

Core ML Tools Python package can be downloaded from: `https://pypi.org/project/coremltools/`

TensorFlow converter can be accessed through the link : `https://github.com/tf-coreml/tf-coreml`

MXNet converter can be downloaded from: `https://github.com/apache/incubator-mxnet/tree/master/tools/coreml`

The Core ML Tools Python package supports conversion from Caffe v1, Keras 1.2.2+, scikit-learn 0.18, XGBoost 0.6, and LIBSVM 3.22 frameworks. This covers models of SVM, tree ensembles, neural networks, generalized linear models, feature engineering, and pipeline models.

You can install Core ML tools through `pip`:

```
pip install -U coremltools
```

Converting your own model into a Core ML model

Convert your existing model into a Core ML model can be done through the `coremltools` Python package. If you want to convert a simple Caffe model to a Core ML model, it can be done with the following example:

```
import coremltools
my_coremlmodel =
   coremltools.converters.caffe.convert('faces.caffemodel')
   coremltools.utils.save_spec(my_coremlmodel, 'faces.mlmodel')
```

This conversion step varies between different models. You may need to add labels and input names, as well as the structure of the model.

Core ML on an iOS app

Integrating Core ML on an iOS app is pretty straightforward. Go and download pre-trained models from the Apple developer page. Download MobileNet model from there.

After you download `MobileNet.mlmodel`, add it to the `Resources` group in your project. The vision framework eases our problems by converting our existing image formats into acceptable input types. You can see the details of your model as shown in the following screenshot. In the upcoming chapters, we will start creating our own models on top of existing models.

Let's look at how to load the model into our application:

Open `ViewController.swift` in your recently created Xcode project, and import both Vision and Core ML frameworks:

```
/**
Lets see the UIImage given to vision framework for the prediction.
The results could be slightly different based on the UIImage conversion.
**/
func visionPrediction(image: UIImage) {
    guard let visionModel = try? VNCoreMLModel(for: model.model) else{
            fatalError("World is gonna crash!")
    }
  let request = VNCoreMLRequest(model: visionModel) { request, error
                                                        in
    if let predictions = request.results as? [VNClassificationObservation]
{
 //top predictions sorted based on confidence
 //results come in string, double tuple
    let topPredictions = observations.prefix(through: 5)
 .map { ($0.identifier, Double($0.confidence)) }
    self.show(results: topPredictions)
    }
  }
}
```

Let's load the same image through the Core ML MobileNet model for the prediction:

```
/**
Method that predicts objects from image using CoreML. The only downside of
this method is, the mlmodel expects images in 224 * 224 pixels resolutions.
So we need to manually convert UIImage
into pixelBuffer.
**/
func coremlPrediction(image: UIImage) {
    if let makeBuffer = image.pixelBuffer(width: 224, height: 224),
    let prediction = try? model.prediction(data: makeBuffer) {
    let topPredictions = top(5, prediction.prob)
    show(results: topPredictions)
    }
}
```

Summary

We are now familiar with the basic idea behind both TensorFlow Lite and Core ML. All the code mentioned in the preceding blocks are completely available in our GitHub repository. Since both of these libraries are running on mobile, they both have limitations. We will dig deeper in further chapters with real-time applications.

In the coming chapters, you will learn how to develop and train specific models based on the specific use case. We will also cover how to build your own mobile application on top of this. Get ready to start training a model and using it on your own mobile app!

2
CNN Based Age and Gender Identification Using Core ML

In this chapter, we are going to build an iOS application to detect the age, gender, and emotion of a person from the camera feed or from the user's photo gallery. We will use existing data models that were built for the same purpose using the Caffe **machine learning** (**ML**) library, and convert those models into Core ML models for the ease of use in our application. We will discuss more how **Convolutional Neural Networks** (**CNNs**) work in terms of predicting age, gender, and emotion with the sample application.

This application can be useful with multiple use cases. A few cases are as follows:

- Finding what kind of photos you capture by parsing all the photos from your gallery
- Understanding the customer entering a location (hospital, restaurant, and so on)
- Figuring out the right marketing data by actually capturing emotions
- Making cars safer by understanding the driver's emotions

There are a lot of other use cases as well. Once you improve accuracy of the data model, you can figure out more and more use cases.

The following topics will be covered in this chapter:

- Age, gender, and emotion prediction
- CNNs
- The implementation of iOS application using Core ML

Age, gender, and emotion prediction

This chapter is going to cover a complete iOS application using Core ML models to detect age, gender, and emotion from a photo taken using an iPhone camera or from a photo in a user's phone gallery.

Core ML enables developers to install and run pre-trained models on a device, and this has its own advantages. Since Core ML lives in the local device, it is not necessary to call a cloud service in order to get the prediction results. This improves the communication latency and also saves data bandwidth. The other crucial benefit of Core ML is privacy. You don't need to send your data to a third party in order to get the results picked for you. The main downside of having an offline model is that the model cannot be updated, and so it cannot be improved with newer inputs. Furthermore, a few models might increase memory footprints, since storage is limited on a mobile device.

With Core ML, when you import the ML model, Xcode will help you to do the rest of the work. In this project, we are going to build the iOS application based on the following research paper by Gil Levi and Tal Hassncer: *Age and gender classification using convolutional neural networks* (`https://ieeexplore.ieee.org/document/7301352`), IEEE Workshop on **Analysis and Modeling of Faces and Gestures (AMFG)**, at the IEEE Conf. on **Computer Vision and Pattern Recognition (CVPR)**, Boston, 2015.

This project is built on a MacBook Pro machine with Xcode version 9.3 on macOS High Sierra. Age and gender prediction became a common application on social media platforms. While there are multiple algorithms for predicting and classifying age and gender, these are still being improved in terms of performance. In this chapter, the classification is done based on deep CNNs.

You can find the application developed in this chapter here: `https://github.com/intrepidkarthi/MLmobileapps/tree/master/Chapter2`. We are going to use Adience dataset for our application in this chapter. This is found here: `https://talhassner.github.io/home/projects/Adience/Adience-data.html`.

Age prediction

There are multiple ways to predict age from a given input photo. Earlier methods work by calculating the ratios between different measurements of facial attributes such as eyes, nose, mouth, and so on. Once facial attributes are calculated based on their size and distance, ratios will be calculated, and age categorization will be done using rule-based engines. Here comes the problem: this method may not work perfectly when we don't have the perfect full frontal face photo that we typically see on a profile picture on any social media platform.

There are multiple ways to predict and identify facial features. One such method is **Gaussian Mixture Models (GMM)**, which were used to represent the distribution of facial patches. We then moved to super vectors and **Hidden Markov Models (HMM)** to represent the facial patch distributions. The best performances were showcased by employing **Local Binary Pattern (LBP)** and the dropout **Support Vector Machine (SVM)** classifier.

Gender prediction

Earlier methods of gender calculation used neural networks. Image intensities and the three-dimensional structure of the face were used to predict gender. SVM classifiers were used for image intensities.

As a general procedure on all upcoming iOS applications, we will look into code signing and provisioning profiles in this chapter. One of the popular benchmarks for this is the FERET benchmark, which uses intensity, shape, and feature to produce near-perfect performance solutions. The dataset that is used in this application uses a complex set of images that are taken from different angles and are exposed to different amounts of light. Another popular benchmark, called **Labeled Faces in the Wild (LFW)**, uses **Local Binary Pattern (LBP)** with an AdaBoost classifier.

Convolutional Neural Networks

One of the earliest applications of neural networks was demonstrated with **Optical Character Recognition (OCR)**, but they were limited by time, computational resources, and other challenges faced when training bigger networks.

CNN is a part of feedforward neural networks, which are influenced by biological processes. This works in the same way that neurons work in the brain, as well as the connectivity patterns between them. These neurons will respond to stimuli that are only in a specific region in the visual field, known as the **receptive field**. When multiple neurons overlap each other, they will cover the whole visual field. The following diagram shows the CNN architecture:

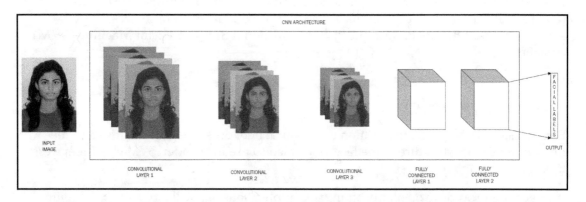

CNN has an input layer and one output layer, as well as multiple hidden layers. These hidden layers consist of pooling layers, convolutional layers, normalization layers, and fully connected layers. Convolutional layers apply a convolution operation and pass the result to the next layer. This resembles how a neuron responds to its visual stimuli. Each neuron will reply to its receptive field only. Deep CNNs are used in various applications, including facial key-point detection, action classification, speech recognition, and so on.

Finding patterns

A very simple approach to identifying a given image containing the number 0 (or not) can be solved by storing images of all the numbers and comparing every image in order to identify a good match. This will be a tricky and tedious process, since computers do math literally. Until we have an exact match of the input image with the one in our repository, we will not find a match. From a computer's perspective, an image will be seen as a two-dimensional array of pixels with a number at every position. Let's see an example of this with the number 0:

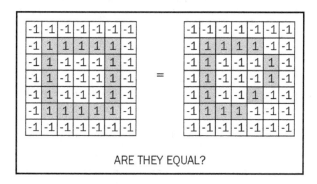

ARE THEY EQUAL?

The diagram on the left within the preceding diagram is in our repository, while the one on the right is the input image, which is a slightly deformed/hand written version of number 0. Upon verification, the computer will try to match all pixel values. However, when there is no exact value match at the pixel level, the number 0 won't be identified. This is where we need a CNN to help.

Finding features from an image

Let's take a look at an image of the letter X. When we feed a new image into the system, the CNN doesn't know whether the feature will match or not. Consequently, it will try to match the feature pattern everywhere across the image. This is how we build a filter:

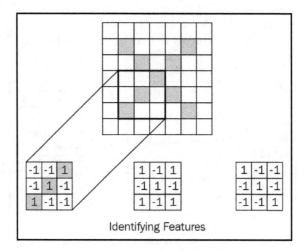

Identifying Features

The math logic we apply here is called **convolution**. To calculate the match of a feature to the portion of the image, multiply each pixel value of the feature by the value of the corresponding pixel in the image. To come to one final value, add together all of the values and divide them by the total number of pixels:

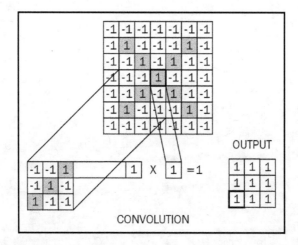

CONVOLUTION

For example, if both pixels are the same color (say a value of 1) then *(1) * (1) = (1)*. If not, then *(-1) * (-1) = 1*. In the end result, every matching pixel will have a resulting value of 1, and every mismatch will have the value of -1.

To complete this convolution process, let's move our feature grid onto the image patch. As shown in the following diagram, the 3 x 3 grid moves the 7 x 7 grid over. This forms the resulting 5 x 5 array. In the resulting grid, the values close to 1 represent strong matches, the values close to 0 represent no match, and the values close to -1 represent photographic negatives of our feature:

-1	-1	-1	-1	-1	-1	-1
-1	-1	-1	-1	-1	-1	-1
-1	-1	-1	-1	-1	-1	-1
-1	-1	-1	-1	-1	-1	-1
-1	-1	-1	-1	-1	-1	-1
-1	-1	-1	-1	-1	-1	-1
-1	-1	-1	-1	-1	-1	-1

X

1	-1	-1
-1	1	-1
-1	-1	1

=

0.77	-0.11	0.33	-0.11	0.33
-0.11	1	-0.33	0.11	-0.11
0.33	-0.33	0.56	-0.33	0.33
-0.11	0.11	-0.33	1	-0.11
0.33	-0.11	0.33	-0.11	0.77

In the next step, we have to repeat the convolution process for all other features. This gives the filtered image—one for each of our filters. In CNN, this is known as the **convolution layer**, and this will be followed by additional layers that are added to it.

This is where CNN gets into heavy computations. This example shows a simple 7 x 7 image that provides 5 x 5 as a result. However, a typical picture will be at least 128 x 128 pixels in size. The computation increases linearly with the number of features, as well as the number of pixels in each feature.

Pooling layer

Another process that makes processing capability efficient is called **pooling**. In the pooling layer, larger images are pushed to shrink in size while keeping the information in them. This is done by sliding a window across the image and taking the maximum value in each window. In a typical pooling layer, a window of 2 or 3 pixels works on a side, but taking steps of 2 pixels also works:

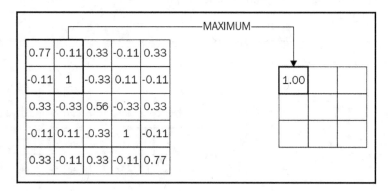

After the pooling layer, the image size will be reduced by one quarter of what it was. This maintains the maximum value from each window. It also preserves the best feature inside every window. This step means that it doesn't care whether the feature fits or not, as long as it fits somewhere inside the window. With the help of this layer, CNN can identify whether a feature exists inside an image, instead of worrying about where it is. In this way, computers need not worry about being literal.

By the end of this layer, bringing down the size of an image from 10 megapixels to 2 megapixels will definitely help us to compute the capability of further processing faster.

Rectified linear units

The logic behind keeping a **rectified linear units** (**ReLUs**) layer is very simple: it replaces all the negative values with 0. This helps us to make CNN mathematically healthier by avoiding negative values:

0.77	-0.11	0.33	-0.11	0.33
-0.11	1	-0.33	0.11	-0.11
0.33	-0.33	0.56	-0.33	0.33
-0.11	0.11	-0.33	1	-0.11
0.33	-0.11	0.33	-0.11	0.77

RELU

0.77	0			

Here, in this layer, the size of the image is not altered. We will get the same size output as the input only when the negative values are replaced by 0.

Local response normalization layer

In biological brain functionality, there is a concept called **lateral inhibition**. This refers to the capacity of one stimulated neuron to bring its neighbors under control. The main agenda for us is to have a local peak value for finding the maximum value in the neighborhood.

This is useful when we are dealing with ReLU neurons. ReLU neurons have unbounded activations, and we need **local response normalization** (**LRN**) to normalize them. To do this, we need to identify high frequency features. By applying LRN, the neurons becomes more sensitive than their neighbors. This is used in an ImageNet ConvNet process, as discussed in the paper mentioned previously.

However, in recent real-time applications, this is given less emphasis as its contributions seem to be very minimal.

Dropout layer

The dropout layer literally refers to dropping a few units of data by ignoring them randomly. This means that contributions to the downstream neurons are removed on the forward pass and the weights are not applied on the backward pass. If the neurons are missing during training, the other neurons will try to make predictions for the missing one. In this manner, neurons will become less effective for specific weights of neurons. We need to do this to avoid overfitting.

Fully connected layer

In this layer, the higher-level layers are taken as the inputs, and the outputs will be votes. For example, we are going to decide whether the given input image contains the letter *a* or *b*. In this step, the inputs are treated as a list, instead of a two-dimensional array. The following diagram shows an example of a fully connected layer:

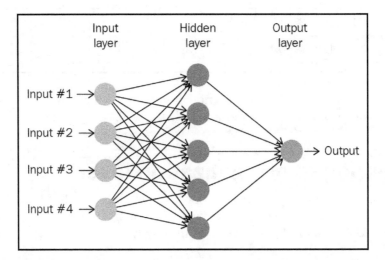

Every value in the list gets its vote to decide whether the given input contains the letter *a* or *b*. Some values will help us to discover whether the given input contains letter *a*, and some values will help us to identify that it contains letter *b*. These specific values will get better votes than the others. Votes are expressed as weights between values and each category of output. CNN drills down to lower layers of the input image till it finds the fully connected layer. The answer with the most votes wins and will be declared as the category of the input.

Let's jump into our case now.

CNNs for age and gender prediction

Some problems may arise when we try to prepare a dataset for age and gender prediction. Creating a dataset from large amounts of social media images might require more of the individual's private data, which may not be available to us. Most of the existing models that are available come with their own limitations. Similarly, overfitting should be taken proper care of, as this is a common problem with CNNs.

Architecture

The network in our application architecture consists of three convolutional layers and two fully connected layers, along with a small amount of neurons.

Here is a flowchart of the CNN, as well as all the components of the completed process:

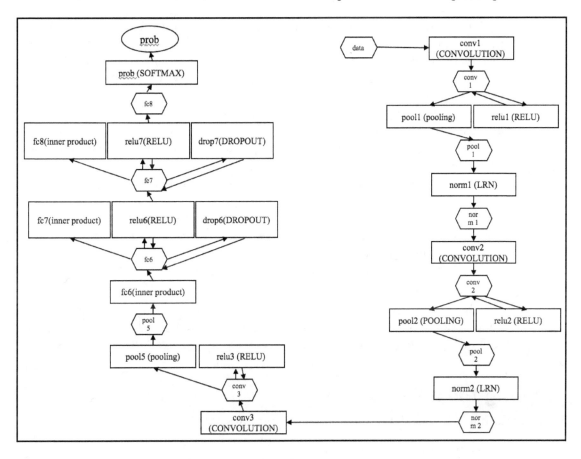

The color channels (red, green, and blue) are processed individually and directly by the network. Whenever an input image is fed in, the size of this image will be scaled to 256 x 256 pixels. After that, 227 x 227 pixels of this new cropped image will be given to the network.

The application developed in this chapter is based on the ImageNet classification applied on 1.2 million images. This paper can be found here: `https://papers.nips.cc/paper/4824-imagenet-classification-with-deep-convolutional-neural-networks.pdf`.

The three subsequent convolutional layers are then defined as follows:

- In the first convolutional layer, 96 filters made up of 3 x 7 x 7 pixels are applied to the cropped input image of 227 x 227 pixel images. This is subsequently followed by a rectified linear unit and a pooling layer. This takes the maximum value of 3 x 3 regions with 2 x 2 pixel strides, followed by an LRN. The output will then be a 96 x 28 x 28 pixel image.
- In the second convolutional layer, 256 filters made up of 96 x 5 x 5 pixels are applied on the input image from the previous layer. This is followed by ReLU, a pooling layer, and an LRN layer. The output contains an image size of 256 x 14 x 14 pixels.
- In the third convolutional layer, 384 filters made up of 256 x 3 x 3 pixels, which is followed by a ReLU and a pooling layer, is applied to the input image from the previous layer. This is then followed by a fully connected layer.
- The fully connected layer is made up of 512 neurons, followed by a ReLU, along with a dropout layer.
- The second fully connected layer is made up of the same 512 neurons, followed by a ReLU, along with a dropout layer.
- The third fully connected layer maps the final section by categorizing age and gender. In the final layer, a softmax function is applied in order to get the probability for each class.

Training the network

Here are the details of the dataset that is used in building this model:

- **Total number of photos**: 26,580
- **Total number of subjects**: 2,284
- **Number of age groups/labels**: 8 (0-2, 4-6, 8-13, 15-20, 25-32, 38-43, 48-53, 60+)
- **Gender labels**: Yes

Initializing the dataset

The weights of all the layers are initiated with random values while maintaining a standard deviation value of 0.01. The network is trained with the previously mentioned training dataset from scratch. The resultant values for the training, represented as binary vectors, correspond to truth classes. This result carries the proper label for the age group classification, as well as the gender truth class associated with it.

The implementation on iOS using Core ML

It is now time to jump into the coding part of the application. We are using a model developed using the Caffe deep learning framework by **Berkeley AI Research** (**BAIR**) team as well as the community of contributors. As a first step, we need to convert the existing Caffe models into Core ML models to be utilized in our application:

```
//Downloading Age and Gender models
wget
  http://www.openu.ac.il/home/hassner/projects/cnn_agegender/cnn_age_gen
        der_models_and_data.0.0.2.zip
unzip -a cnn_age_gender_models_and_data.0.0.2.zip
```

Now, go to the extracted folder and convert the model into a Core ML model:

```
import coremltools

folder = 'cnn_age_gender_models_and_data.0.0.2'

coreml_model = coremltools.converters.caffe.convert(
  (folder + '/age_net.caffemodel', folder + '/deploy_age.prototxt'),
   image_input_names = 'data',
   class_labels = 'ages.txt'
)

coreml_model.save('Age.mlmodel')
```

The same needs to be done for the gender model as well. To kick start our work, let's create our first Core ML application.

Let's select **Single View App** from the initial screen, illustrated in this screenshot:

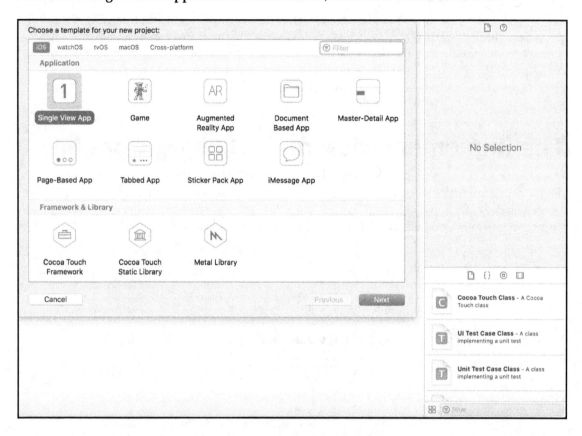

On the next wizard screen, pick an appropriate name for your application. Fill in the rest of the fields, including the organization name, as well as the identifier. We are not going to use core data in this application, so let's skip that option. Let's start by creating a new app in Xcode. The following screenshot depicts how to create a new project in Xcode:

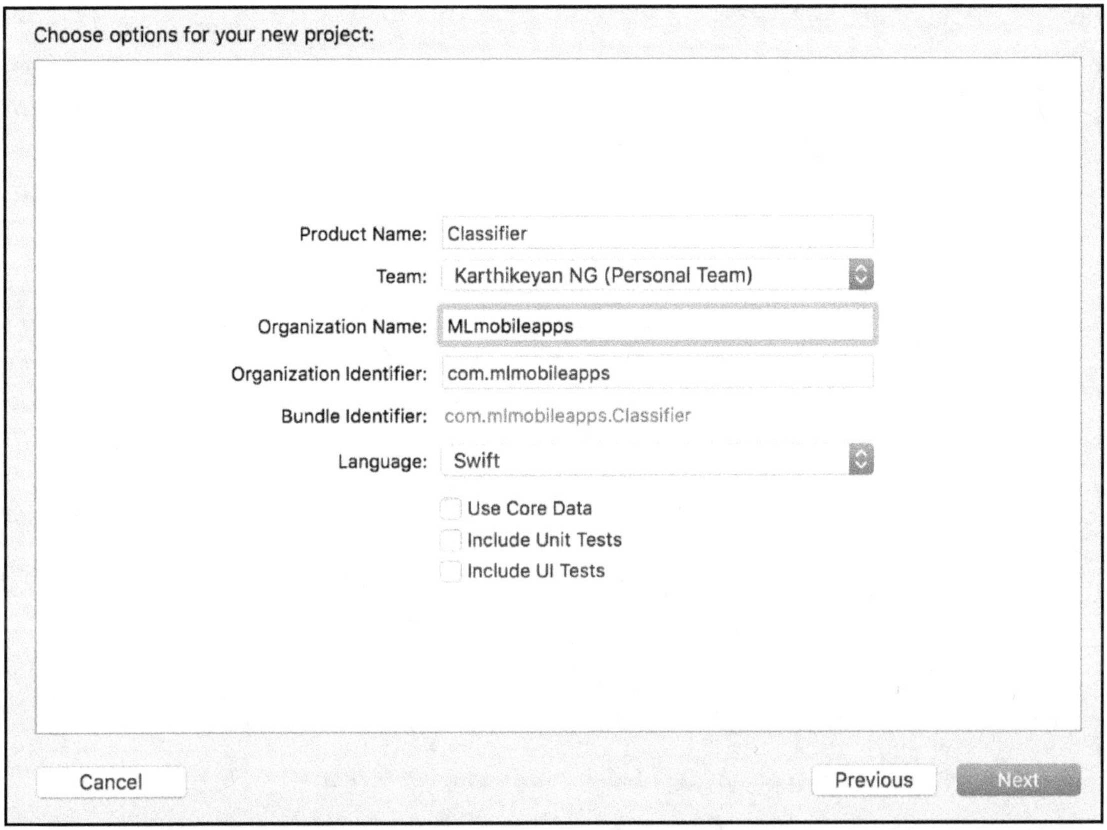

Choose options for your new project:

Product Name:	Classifier
Team:	Karthikeyan NG (Personal Team)
Organization Name:	MLmobileapps
Organization Identifier:	com.mlmobileapps
Bundle Identifier:	com.mlmobileapps.Classifier
Language:	Swift

 Use Core Data
 Include Unit Tests
 Include UI Tests

Cancel   Previous   Next

Once you select the file location in which to save your application, you will be able to see the general information on the new application that has been initialized, as shown in the following screenshot:

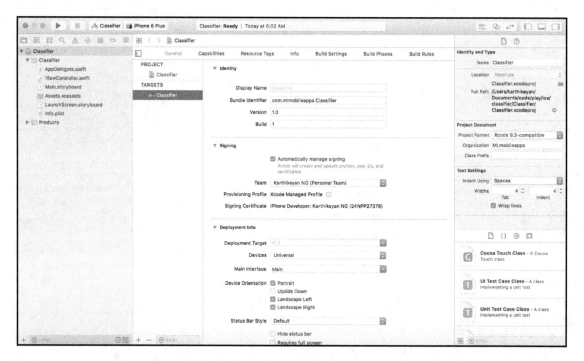

Let's start by creating a controller for picking an image from the mobile's gallery or the camera.

The following code block creates a controller for the image picker:

```
import UIKit

open class ImageClassificationController<Service:
        ClassificationServiceProtocol>: UIViewController,
        PhotoSourceControllerDelegate, UINavigationControllerDelegate,
        UIImagePickerControllerDelegate {
            /// View with image, button and labels
        public private(set) lazy var mainView =
                        ImageClassificationView(frame: .zero)
        /// Service used to perform gender, age and emotion classification
        public let classificationService: Service = .init()
        /// Status bar style
        open override var preferredStatusBarStyle: UIStatusBarStyle {
        return .lightContent
```

```swift
    }

// MARK: - View lifecycle
 open override func viewDidLoad() {
     super.viewDidLoad()
     mainView.frame = view.bounds
     mainView.button.setTitle("Select a photo", for: .normal)
     mainView.button.addTarget(self, action:
#selector(handleSelectPhotoTap), for: .touchUpInside)
     view.addSubview(mainView)

    mainView.setupConstraints()
        classificationService.setup()
    }

    open override func viewDidLayoutSubviews() {
        super.viewDidLayoutSubviews()
        mainView.frame = view.bounds
    }

// MARK: - Actions
 /// Present image picker
 @objc private func handleSelectPhotoTap() {
 let sourcePicker = PhotoSourceController()
 sourcePicker.delegate = self
 present(sourcePicker, animated: true)
 }

// MARK: - PhotoSourceControllerDelegate
 public func photoSourceController(_ controller: PhotoSourceController,
   didSelectSourceType sourceType: UIImagePickerControllerSourceType) {
 let imagePicker = UIImagePickerController()
 imagePicker.delegate = self
 imagePicker.allowsEditing = true
 imagePicker.sourceType = sourceType
 present(imagePicker, animated: true)
 }

// MARK: - UIImagePickerControllerDelegate
 public func imagePickerController(_ picker: UIImagePickerController,
        didFinishPickingMediaWithInfo info: [String : Any]) {
 let editedImage = info[UIImagePickerControllerEditedImage] as? UIImage
 guard let image = editedImage, let ciImage = CIImage(image: image) else {
 print("Can't analyze selected photo")
 return
 }

DispatchQueue.main.async { [weak mainView] in
```

```
mainView?.imageView.image = image
mainView?.label.text = ""
}

picker.dismiss(animated: true)

// Run Core ML classifier
DispatchQueue.global(qos: .userInteractive).async { [weak self] in
self?.classificationService.classify(image: ciImage)
}
}
}
```

In the controller, once the image is picked, we will pass it to the next page where we classify the image. The picker controller should look as follows:

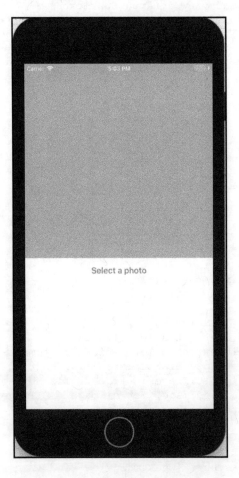

Now, let's add an image source picker that allows the user to pick an image from the photo gallery, as well as from the camera:

```swift
import UIKit

/// Delegate protocol used for `PhotoSourceController`
  public protocol PhotoSourceControllerDelegate: class {
 /// Sent to the delegate when a photo source was selected
 func photoSourceController(_ controller: PhotoSourceController,
 didSelectSourceType sourceType: UIImagePickerControllerSourceType)
 }


/// Controller used to present a picker where the user can select a
/// source for a photo
public final class PhotoSourceController: UIAlertController {
 /// The controller's delegate
 public weak var delegate: PhotoSourceControllerDelegate?
public override func viewDidLoad() {
 super.viewDidLoad()
 addAction(forSourceType: .camera, title: "Snap a photo")
 addAction(forSourceType: .savedPhotosAlbum, title: "Photo Album")
 addCancelAction()
 }
 }

// MARK: - Actions

private extension PhotoSourceController {
 func addAction(forSourceType sourceType:
UIImagePickerControllerSourceType, title: String) {
 let action = UIAlertAction(title: title, style: .default) { [weak
                        self] _ in
 guard let `self` = self else {
 return
 }
 self.delegate?.photoSourceController(self, didSelectSourceType:
                                sourceType)
 }
addAction(action)
 }

func addCancelAction() {
 let action = UIAlertAction(title: "Cancel", style: .cancel, handler:
                        nil)
 addAction(action)
 }
 }
```

When the user clicks on the **Select a photo** option, it brings up options to **Snap a photo** from the mobile's camera or pick an image from the user's **Photo Album**. There is also an option to **Cancel** the popup. The following screenshot depicts the image selection menu for the gallery:

Our final task is to add actions to the image selection menu items. Once the picture is selected, the corresponding methods are called to fetch the results from the model.

The following code block is used to add functions to the buttons added:

```
extension ViewController: ClassificationServiceDelegate {
  func classificationService(_ service: ClassificationService,
  didDetectGender gender: String) {
  append(to: mainView.label, title: "Gender", text: gender)
  }

  func classificationService(_ service: ClassificationService, didDetectAge
  age: String) {
  append(to: mainView.label, title: "Age", text: age)
  }

  func classificationService(_ service: ClassificationService,
  didDetectEmotion emotion: String) {
  append(to: mainView.label, title: "Emotions", text: emotion)
  }


  /// Set results of the classification request
  func append(to label: UILabel, title: String, text: String) {
  DispatchQueue.main.async { [weak label] in
  let attributedText = label?.attributedText ?? NSAttributedString(string:
  "")
  let string = NSMutableAttributedString(attributedString: attributedText)
  string.append(.init(string: "\(title): ", attributes: [.font:
  UIFont.boldSystemFont(ofSize: 25)]))
  string.append(.init(string: text, attributes: [.font:
  UIFont.systemFont(ofSize: 25)]))
  string.append(.init(string: "\n\n"))
  label?.attributedText = string
  }
  }
```

The methods used here get the results for gender, age, and emotion from the classification service and pass it on to the UI. The result may not be 100% accurate, as the model runs on your local system. The following screenshot depicts the complete functionality of the application that shows information related to the image:

Summary

In this chapter, we learned to build a complete iOS application from scratch. We also learned how to convert a Caffe model into a Core ML model. Now we know how to import a Core ML model into an iOS app and get the predicted results from the model. By doing this, we save data bandwidth without using the internet, and the data remains on a local device without affecting user privacy.

In the next chapter, with this knowledge, we'll move on to building an application to apply an artistic style to an existing image through neural networks.

3
Applying Neural Style Transfer on Photos

In this chapter, we are going to build a complete iOS and Android application in which image transformations are applied to our own images in a fashion similar to the Instagram app. For this application, we are going to use Core ML and TensorFlow models again with the help of TensorFlow. To make this work, we will have to perform some small hacks.

The best use case for this chapter is based on a photo-editing app called **Prisma** with which you can convert your images into paintings using neural networks. You can convert your image into an art form that looks like it was painted by Picasso or Salvador Dali.

In this chapter, we will cover topics on:

- Artistic neural style transfer
- Building application using neural style transfer

Artistic neural style transfer

Image transformations are applied through fast style transfer. Let's dig deeper into how style transfer works before the implementation of our mobile application. Everyone loves to see their work in an artistic style. Artistic neural style transfer helps us see our own images in an art form that involves mixing your content and a style in order to introduce a unique visual experience. Before now, there was no AI-based system capable of implementing such a system.

Look at the following screenshot for an example of how an artistic style is applied on a normal image:

The application we will be creating in this chapter is based on the implementation of a system similar to that shown in the preceding screenshot. There have been multiple papers published that prove its near-human performance of facial and object recognition. Deep neural networks help to implement artificial human vision. In this application, the algorithm that we use implements a deep neural network that creates images with high visual quality. The neural network is used to bifurcate and rearrange the content and style of input images. In that way, it provides a neural logic to create artistic images.

 This project is based on the following paper: https://arxiv.org/pdf/ 1508.06576.pdf and the GitHub project here: https://github.com/ lengstrom/fast-style-transfer. Another paper on near-human facial recognition can be found at the following link: https://ieeexplore. ieee.org/document/6909616/.

Background

In neural networks, **Convolutional Neural Networks** (**CNNs**) are one major technique that is being used widely for image classifications, object detection, facial recognition, and so on. A typical CNN algorithm takes an image as an input in an array format and produces its classification as output, for example, a head shot picture of a person of 256 * 256 * 3 (height * width * dimension) an array of matrix of RGB values. Here the number 3 refers to RGB values.

In a typical transfer algorithm, more focus would be given on object recognition, and a CNN would be trained in object recognition. In the CNN processing hierarchy, when the processing level increases, the object information becomes more explicit on higher layers. The transformation in each processing layer improves object recognition by finding the actual content in the image rather than computing detailed pixel values. Higher layers in the processing of CNN always represent the identified object and their arrangements, while lower layers represent more information on deeper pixel values in order to reproduce the image.

As shown in the following, to figure out the style of the input image, we design a feature space that helps us capture texture-related information. This space is based on the filter responses in each layer of the network, while the multiple layers contain a feature correlation that helps to build multiple variations of the input image on a different scale. In this way, it captures the texture information but doesn't involve global arrangements of the object:

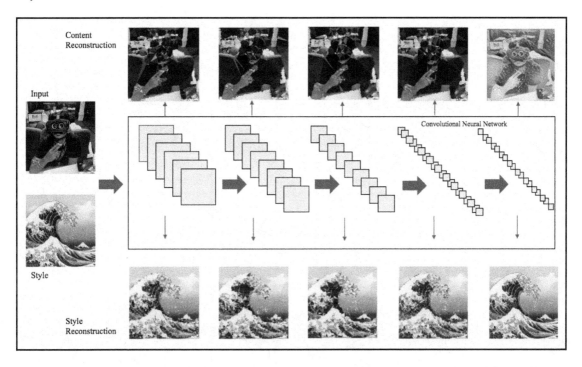

In the preceding screenshot, which depicts a CNN process, filters are applied to each step. The number of filters increases as the size of the filtered image reduces. Size reduction happens through down-sampling mechanisms such as pooling. In the CNN layers, the image can be reconstructed at a particular stage, depending on the input to the network. This information can also be visualized at different processing stages in the CNN. This is done by reconstructing the input image, based on the network's responses in a particular layer. As shown in the preceding screenshot, the content can be recreated at each step without waiting till the final step. Let's take a closer look at the **Visual Geometry Group** (**VGG**) network dataset.

VGG network

A VGG network can detect 1,000 objects inside a given input image. This takes image inputs of 224 * 244 * 3 in size (the number 3 represents RGB values). This is built using convolutional layers of 3 x 3 in size with a total of 16 layers. It also provides a Top-1 accuracy of 70.5% and a Top-5 accuracy of 90%.

Layers in the VGG network

There are 16 layers in the VGG network, explained as follows:

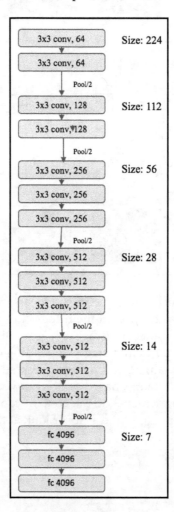

The pre-trained VGG TensorFlow model link can be found here: `https://www.cs.toronto.edu/~frossard/vgg16/vgg16_weights.npz`.

We can visualize and build the image with the information captured by the style feature outputs on each layer. We can find texturized images in terms of localized structure and colors. As you can see in the previous image, the complexity and visualization of the localized image structure increases along the hierarchy, while it loses pixel clarity.

Neural style transfer shows that style and content in CNN can be separated, allowing us to manipulate and produce meaningful outputs. The example it uses is the content representation of a photograph showing several well-known paintings taken from different periods of art, as shown in the following screenshot:

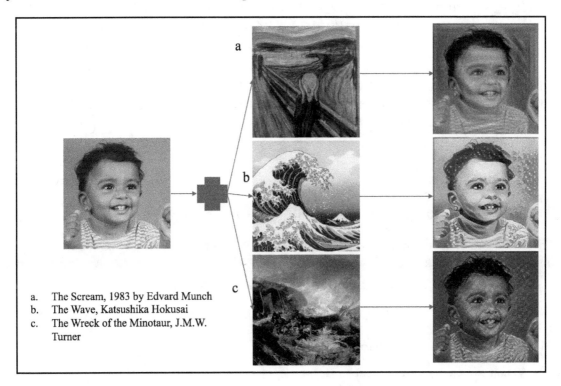

a. The Scream, 1983 by Edvard Munch
b. The Wave, Katsushika Hokusai
c. The Wreck of the Minotaur, J.M.W. Turner

Of course, the image content and the style cannot be independent of each other completely. When applying CNN, the content of one image is processed with the style of another image where we will not see one perfect image that matches both constraints. We can do a trade-off between the content and style to create appealing output images.

In our example, we have rendered photographs with well known paintings. This method is called **non-photo realistic rendering**.

Building the applications

Here comes the app building section of the chapter. When building this application, we are going to use fast style transfers on pre-trained models. We can also use customized models with adjustments to make the app work on the iOS platform.

The following are two examples on style transfer implementation that use TensorFlow: `https://github.com/titu1994/Neural-Style-Transfer` and `https://github.com/yining1023/fast_style_transfer_in_ML5/`.

As a consequence of this, we are going to make use of the TensorFlow-to-Core ML library 1.1.0+ in this tutorial. The GitHub link to this is as follows: `https://github.com/tf-coreml/tf-coreml`, and the dependencies are listed as follows:

- `tensorflow` >= 1.5.0
- `coremltools` >= 0.8
- `numpy` >= 1.6.2
- `protobuf` >= 3.1.0
- `six` >= 1.10.0

To get the latest version of the TensorFlow-to-Core ML converter, clone this repository and install it from the source as follows:

```
git clone https://github.com/tf-coreml/tf-coreml.git
cd tf-coreml
pip install -e
```

Alternatively, you can run the following:

```
python setup.py bdist_wheel
```

To install the PyPI package, run the following:

```
pip install -U tfcoreml
```

Now, let's start with the preliminary steps. This is necessary since fast style transfer is not meant for a production-level application:

1. As a first step, we need to figure out the name of the output node for our graph. TensorFlow auto-generates this, and we can get it by printing the net in the evaluate.py script. We use the following block to get the output node name:

```
# function ffwd, line 93
# https://github.com/lengstrom/fast-style-
transfer/blob/master/evaluate.py#L93
preds = transform.net(img_placeholder)
# Printing the output node name
print(preds)
```

2. After we have done this, we can run the script to see the printed output. We are using the pre-trained wave model here. The following code block gives you the output node name:

```
$ python evaluate.py --checkpoint wave.ckpt --in-path inputs/ --
out-
    path outputs/

> Tensor("add_37:0", shape=(20, 720, 884, 3), dtype=float32,
    device=/device:GPU:0)
```

The output node name is the important data here, and is add_37. This makes sense as the last unnamed operator in the net is addition, as shown in the preceding code block:

```
#https://github.com/lengstrom/fast-style-transfer/blob/master/src/t
ransform.py#L17
preds = tf.nn.tanh(conv_t3) * 150 + 255./2
```

3. Let's make a few more changes to evaluate.py and save the graph to a disk:

```
#
https://github.com/lengstrom/fast-style-transfer/blob/master/evalua
te.py#L98
if os.path.isdir(checkpoint_dir):
    ckpt = tf.train.get_checkpoint_state(checkpoint_dir)
    if ckpt and ckpt.model_checkpoint_path:
        saver.restore(sess, ckpt.model_checkpoint_path)
        ########## for pre-trained models ###########
        frozen_graph_def =
tf.graph_util.convert_variables_to_constants(sess,sess.graph_def,
                                            ['add_37'])
        with open('output_graph.pb', 'wb') as f:
```

```
            f.write(frozen_graph_def.SerializeToString())
        ######################################################
    else:
       raise Exception("No checkpoint found...")
    else:
            saver.restore(sess, checkpoint_dir)
            ########## for custom models ##########
            frozen_graph_def =
    tf.graph_util.convert_variables_to_constants(sess,sess.graph_def,
                                        ['add_37'])
            with open('output_graph.pb', 'wb') as f:
                f.write(frozen_graph_def.SerializeToString())
        ######################################################
```

4. Now, we run `evaluate.py` on a model, and we will end up with our graph file saved:

```
$ python evaluate.py --checkpoint wave/wave.ckpt --in-path inputs/
-
    -out-path outputs/ --device "/cpu:0" --batch-size 1
```

We will get the `output_graph.pb` file as output and we can move on to the Core ML conversion part.

TensorFlow-to-Core ML conversion

TensorFlow-to-CoreML conversion is done using the `tf-coreml` library.

 Check out the TensorFlow-to-Core ML convertor library at the following link: `https://github.com/tf-coreml/tf-coreml`.

We have a three steps process for converting a TensorFlow model to Core ML.

1. The model we generated (`output_graph.pb`) in the last step requires support for *power*. Apple's Core ML tools provide a unary conversion which supports *power*. We need to add this code into the TensorFlow implementation as follows:

```
# tfcoreml src

# file1 : _interpret_shapes.py

# in the _SHAPE_TRANSLATOR_REGISTRY we need to add the Pow
operation
```

```
_SHAPE_TRANSLATOR_REGISTRY = {
    ... previous keys ...
  # add this:
  'Pow': _identity,
}


# file 2: _ops_to_layers.py

# in the _OP_REGISTRY to add the Pow operation
_OP_REGISTRY = {
    ... previous keys ...
  # add this:
  'Pow': _layers.pow
}


# file 3: _layers.py

# in the _layers we need to define the conversion
def pow(op, context):
    const_name = compat.as_bytes(op.inputs[1].name)
    const_val = context.consts[const_name]
## Note: this is .5 here, you can play around with this
    input_name = compat.as_bytes(op.inputs[0].name)
    output_name = compat.as_bytes(op.outputs[0].name)
    context.builder.add_unary(output_name, input_name, output_name,
                              'power', alpha=const_val)
    context.translated[output_name] = True
```

2. Create and run the conversion script:

```
import tfcoreml as tf_converter
tf_converter.convert(tf_model_path = 'output_graph.pb',
                     mlmodel_path = 'model_name.mlmodel',
                     output_feature_names = ['add_37:0'],
                     image_input_names = ['img_placeholder__0'])


$ python convert.py
```

The actual Core ML converter does not provide the capability to output images from a model as of now.

3. Create and run the output transform script on the model (`own_model.mlmodel`), which was the preceding output:

```
import coremltools

def convert_multiarray_output_to_image(spec, feature_name,
                                       is_bgr=False):
    """
    Convert an output multiarray to be represented as an image
    This will modify the Model spec passed in.
    """


    for output in spec.description.output:
        if output.name != feature_name:
            continue
        if output.type.WhichOneof('Type') != 'multiArrayType':
            raise ValueError("%s is not a multiarray type" %
                             output.name)
        array_shape = tuple(output.type.multiArrayType.shape)
        channels, height, width = array_shape
        from coremltools.proto import FeatureTypes_pb2 as ft
        if channels == 1:
            output.type.imageType.colorSpace =
                ft.ImageFeatureType.ColorSpace.Value('GRAYSCALE')
        elif channels == 3:
            if is_bgr:
                output.type.imageType.colorSpace =
                    ft.ImageFeatureType.ColorSpace.Value('BGR')
            else:
                output.type.imageType.colorSpace =
                    ft.ImageFeatureType.ColorSpace.Value('RGB')
        else:
            raise ValueError("Channel Value %d not supported for
                              image inputs" % channels)
        output.type.imageType.width = width
        output.type.imageType.height = height


model = coremltools.models.MLModel('own_model.mlmodel')
spec = model.get_spec()
convert_multiarray_output_to_image(spec,'add_37__0',is_bgr=False)
newModel = coremltools.models.MLModel(spec)
newModel.save('wave.mlmodel')
```

Now run the following code:

```
$ python output.py
```

Now we have our own ML model.

iOS application

In the iOS application, we will cover the important details here:

1. Import the models into your Xcode project. Make sure you add them to the target.
2. After importing, you'll be able to instantiate the models like so:

```
private let models = [
    wave().model,
    udnie().model,
    rain_princess().model,
    la_muse().model
]
```

3. Create a class for the model input parameter, which is MLFeatureProvider. img_placeholder is the input that is defined in the evaluation script:

```
//  StyleTransferInput.swift
//  StyleTransfer

import CoreML

class StyleTransferInput : MLFeatureProvider {
    var input: CVPixelBuffer
    var featureNames: Set<String> {
        get {
            return ["img_placeholder__0"]
        }
    }
    func featureValue(for featureName: String) -> MLFeatureValue? {
        if (featureName == "img_placeholder__0") {
            return MLFeatureValue(pixelBuffer: input)
        }
        return nil
    }
    init(input: CVPixelBuffer) {
        self.input = input
```

```
            }
        }
```

4. Now, call the model for the desired output:

```
private func stylizeImage(cgImage: CGImage, model: MLModel) ->
CGImage {
    // size can change here if you want, remember to run right
sizes
        in the fst evaluating script
    let input = StyleTransferInput(input: pixelBuffer(cgImage:
                            cgImage, width: 883, height: 720))

    // model.prediction will run the style model on input image
    let outFeatures = try! model.prediction(from: input)
    // we get the image buffer after
    let output = outFeatures.featureValue(for:
                        "add_37__0")!.imageBufferValue!
    // remaining code to convert image buffer here .....
}
```

You can pull the code directly from the GitHub repository here: https://
github.com/intrepidkarthi/MLmobileapps/tree/master/Chapter3
and https://github.com/PacktPublishing/Machine-Learning-
Projects-for-Mobile-Applications.

Android application

Let's jump into building an Android application using a TensorFlow model. In this case, we will use the pre-built model from Google featuring style transfer.

The basic functionality of this application is going to be similar to applying a filter on Instagram. We will either take a picture using the camera or select a file from the mobile gallery and apply the artistic style transfer on top of the image from the list of designs available.

Setting up the model

The model is part of a TensorFlow research project called **Magenta**. It mainly involves applying **machine learning** (**ML**) to the process of creating music and art. This involves developing new algorithms using reinforcement learning and deep learning, which can be applied on music files and images, building tools that will help artists and musicians.

 The repository for the TensorFlow research project can be found here: `https://github.com/tensorflow/magenta`.

You can skip this section on setting up the model if you are downloading our repository, which already has the model file ready.

Style transfer is the process in which the combination of a content image and a style image produces a resulting pastiche image. This is discussed in detail in the paper *A Learned Representation for Artistic Style* by Vincent Dumoulin, Jon Shlens, and Manjunath Kudlur (`https://arxiv.org/abs/1610.07629`).

We can either use an existing model or we can set up our own model for use in our application. To do this, we need to set up the Magenta environment first. It is simple to install this on a Mac using an automated script. If you are setting up in another environment, please check the manual installation details at the Magenta project.

Run the following command on the Terminal to install Magenta:

```
curl
    https://raw.githubusercontent.com/tensorflow/magenta/master/magenta/
            tools/magenta-install.sh > /tmp/magenta-install.sh

bash /tmp/magenta-install.sh
```

Now, open a new Terminal window and run the following:

```
source activate magenta
```

We are now able to use Magenta!

There are two pre-trained models available. Let's use the one called **Monet**.

To download this, the following is the link to the model: `http://download.magenta.tensorflow.org/models/multistyle-pastiche-generator-monet.ckpt`.

Run the following command:

```
$ image_stylization_transform \
    --num_styles=<NUMBER_OF_STYLES> \
    --which_styles="[0,1,2,5,14]" \
    --checkpoint=/path/to/model.ckpt \
    --input_image=/path/to/image.jpg \
    --output_dir=/tmp/image_stylization/output \
    --output_basename="stylized"
```

You should pass the correct model number in the argument. For Monet, this is `10`. The `which_styles` argument specifies a list of the linear combination of styles that is applied on a single image. The following is an example that applies the Monet style:

```
$ image_stylization_transform \
    --num_styles=10 \
    --checkpoint=multistyle-pastiche-generator-monet.ckpt \
    --which_styles="
            {0:0.1,1:0.1,2:0.1,3:0.1,4:0.1,5:0.1,6:0.1,
            7:0.1,8:0.1,9:0.1}" \
    --input_image=photo.jpg \
    --output_dir=/tmp/image_stylization/output \
    --output_basename="all_monet_styles"
```

Training your own model

You can train your model with your own style images. This can be done in three steps.

Get ready with your own style images in a directory and download the trained VGG model checkpoint from here: `http://download.tensorflow.org/models/vgg_16_2016_08_28.tar.gz`:

```
//Setting up your own images
$ image_stylization_create_dataset \
  --vgg_checkpoint=/path/to/vgg_16.ckpt \
  --style_files=/path/to/style/images/*.jpg \
  --output_file=/tmp/image_stylization/style_images.tfrecord
```

Then, you can start training the model:

```
//Training a model
$ image_stylization_train \
 --train_dir=/tmp/image_stylization/run1/train
 --style_dataset_file=/tmp/image_stylization/style_images.tfrecord \
 --num_styles=<NUMBER_OF_STYLES> \
 --vgg_checkpoint=/path/to/vgg_16.ckpt \
 --imagenet_data_dir=/path/to/imagenet-2012-tfrecord
```

After this, evaluate your training:

```
$ image_stylization_evaluate \
 --style_dataset_file=/tmp/image_stylization/style_images.tfrecord \
 --num_styles=<NUMBER_OF_STYLES> \
 --train_dir=/tmp/image_stylization/run1/train \
 --eval_dir=/tmp/image_stylization/run1/eval \
 --vgg_checkpoint=/path/to/vgg_16.ckpt \
 --imagenet_data_dir=/path/to/imagenet-2012-tfrecord \
 --style_grid
```

Or, if you want to fine-tune an existing model, enter the following:

```
$ image_stylization_finetune \
 --checkpoint=/path/to/model.ckpt \
 --train_dir=/tmp/image_stylization/run2/train \
 --style_dataset_file=/tmp/image_stylization/style_images.tfrecord \
 --num_styles=<NUMBER_OF_STYLES> \
 --vgg_checkpoint=/path/to/vgg_16.ckpt \
 --imagenet_data_dir=/path/to/imagenet-2012-tfrecord
```

Putting this together, we are left with the following:

```
# Select an image (any jpg or png).
input_image = 'evaluation_image/hero.jpg'

image = np.expand_dims(image_utils.load_np_image(
                    os.path.expanduser(input_image)), 0)

checkpoint = 'checkpoints/multistyle-pastiche-generator-monet.ckpt'
              num_styles = 10
# Number of images in checkpoint file. Do not change.
# Styles from checkpoint file to render. They are done in batch, so the #
more rendered, the longer it will take and the more memory will be
# used.These can be modified as you like. Here we randomly select six
# styles.
styles = range(num_styles)
random.shuffle(styles)
which_styles = styles[0:6]
```

```
num_rendered = len(which_styles)

with tf.Graph().as_default(), tf.Session() as sess:
    stylized_images = model.transform(
        tf.concat([image for _ in range(len(which_styles))], 0),
        normalizer_params={
            'labels': tf.constant(which_styles),
            'num_categories': num_styles,
            'center': True,
            'scale': True})
    model_saver = tf.train.Saver(tf.global_variables())
    model_saver.restore(sess, checkpoint)
    stylized_images = stylized_images.eval()
    # Plot the images.
    counter = 0
    num_cols = 3
    f, axarr = plt.subplots(num_rendered // num_cols, num_cols,
                                            figsize=(25, 25))
    for col in range(num_cols):
        for row in range( num_rendered // num_cols):
            axarr[row, col].imshow(stylized_images[counter])
            axarr[row, col].set_xlabel('Style %i' % which_styles[counter])
            counter += 1
```

Now, let's start building the Android application. In this application, we will use the TensorFlow model built using the following network code from the Magenta project:

```
"""Style transfer network code."""

from __future__ import absolute_import
from __future__ import division
from __future__ import print_function


import tensorflow as tf

from magenta.models.image_stylization import ops

slim = tf.contrib.slim


def transform(input_, normalizer_fn=ops.conditional_instance_norm,
              normalizer_params=None, reuse=False):
  """Maps content images to stylized images.

  Args:
    input_: Tensor. Batch of input images.
    normalizer_fn: normalization layer function.  Defaults to
```

```
        ops.conditional_instance_norm.
    normalizer_params: dict of parameters to pass to the conditional
                       instance
        normalization op.
    reuse: bool. Whether to reuse model parameters. Defaults to False.

  Returns:
    Tensor. The output of the transformer network.
  """
  if normalizer_params is None:
    normalizer_params = {'center': True, 'scale': True}
  with tf.variable_scope('transformer', reuse=reuse):
    with slim.arg_scope(
        [slim.conv2d],
        activation_fn=tf.nn.relu,
        normalizer_fn=normalizer_fn,
        normalizer_params=normalizer_params,
        weights_initializer=tf.random_normal_initializer(0.0, 0.01),
        biases_initializer=tf.constant_initializer(0.0)):
      with tf.variable_scope('contract'):
        h = conv2d(input_, 9, 1, 32, 'conv1')
        h = conv2d(h, 3, 2, 64, 'conv2')
        h = conv2d(h, 3, 2, 128, 'conv3')
      with tf.variable_scope('residual'):
        h = residual_block(h, 3, 'residual1')
        h = residual_block(h, 3, 'residual2')
        h = residual_block(h, 3, 'residual3')
        h = residual_block(h, 3, 'residual4')
        h = residual_block(h, 3, 'residual5')
      with tf.variable_scope('expand'):
        h = upsampling(h, 3, 2, 64, 'conv1')
        h = upsampling(h, 3, 2, 32, 'conv2')
        return upsampling(h, 9, 1, 3, 'conv3', activation_fn=tf.nn.sigmoid)
```

Let's explore the same-padded convolution with mirror padding instead of zero-padding. `conv2d` function expects `'kernel_size'` to be odd:

```
def conv2d(input_,
           kernel_size,
           stride,
           num_outputs,
           scope,
  activation_fn=tf.nn.relu):
  """
  Args:
  input_: 4-D Tensor input.
  kernel_size: int (odd-valued) representing the kernel size.
  stride: int representing the strides.
```

```
num_outputs: int. Number of output feature maps.
scope: str. Scope under which to operate.
activation_fn: activation function.
Returns:
4-D Tensor output.
Raises:
ValueError: if `kernel_size` is even.
"""
if kernel_size % 2 == 0:
raise ValueError('kernel_size is expected to be odd.')
padding = kernel_size // 2
padded_input = tf.pad(
input_, [[0, 0], [padding, padding], [padding, padding], [0, 0]],
mode='REFLECT')
return slim.conv2d(
padded_input,
padding='VALID',
kernel_size=kernel_size,
stride=stride,
num_outputs=num_outputs,
activation_fn=activation_fn,
scope=scope)
```

Now, let's see the smooth replacement of a same-padded transposed convolution. This function first computes a nearest-neighbor upsampling of the input by a factor of 'stride', then applies a mirror-padded, same-padded convolution. It expects 'kernel_size' to be odd:

```
def upsampling(input_,
               kernel_size,
               stride,
               num_outputs,
               scope,
activation_fn=tf.nn.relu):
"""
Args:
input_: 4-D Tensor input.
kernel_size: int (odd-valued) representing the kernel size.
stride: int representing the strides.
num_outputs: int. Number of output feature maps.
scope: str. Scope under which to operate.
activation_fn: activation function.
Returns:
4-D Tensor output.
Raises:
ValueError: if `kernel_size` is even.
"""
if kernel_size % 2 == 0:
```

```
raise ValueError('kernel_size is expected to be odd.')
with tf.variable_scope(scope):
shape = tf.shape(input_)
height = shape[1]
width = shape[2]
upsampled_input = tf.image.resize_nearest_neighbor(
input_, [stride * height, stride * width])
return conv2d(
upsampled_input,
kernel_size,
1,
num_outputs,
'conv',
activation_fn=activation_fn)
```

A residual block made of two mirror-padded, same-padded convolutions.
residual_block function expects 'kernel_size' to be odd:

```
def residual_block(input_, kernel_size, scope, activation_fn=tf.nn.relu):
    """
    Args:
    input_: 4-D Tensor, the input.
    kernel_size: int (odd-valued) representing the kernel size.
    scope: str, scope under which to operate.
    activation_fn: activation function.
    Returns:
    4-D Tensor, the output.
    Raises:
    ValueError: if `kernel_size` is even.
    """
    if kernel_size % 2 == 0:
    raise ValueError('kernel_size is expected to be odd.')
    with tf.variable_scope(scope):
    num_outputs = input_.get_shape()[-1].value
    h_1 = conv2d(input_, kernel_size, 1, num_outputs, 'conv1', activation_fn)
    h_2 = conv2d(h_1, kernel_size, 1, num_outputs, 'conv2', None)
    return input_ + h_2
```

Now, we are good to start building the Android application.

Building the application

This application is compiled with the following dependency for TensorFlow, which will pull the latest version:

```
allprojects {
 repositories {
 jcenter()
 }
}
dependencies {
 compile 'org.tensorflow:tensorflow-android:+'
}
```

We will create a `.CameraActivity`, which will be the launcher activity of the application. This is defined in the `AndroidManifest.xml` file:

```
<activity android:name=".CameraActivity"
    android:icon="@mipmap/ic_launcher">
    <intent-filter>
        <action android:name="android.intent.action.MAIN" />
        <category android:name="android.intent.category.LAUNCHER" />
    </intent-filter>
</activity>
```

Setting up the camera and an image picker

In the `.CameraActivity`, we will use the camera module from the `CameraKit` library found at the following link: `https://github.com/CameraKit/camerakit-android`.

To start capturing the image, we will start by initializing the `CameraView` object:

```
myCamera = findViewById(R.id.camera);
myCamera.setPermissions(CameraKit.Constants.PERMISSIONS_PICTURE);
myCamera.setMethod(CameraKit.Constants.METHOD_STILL);
myCamera.setJpegQuality(70);
myCamera.setCropOutput(true);
```

When you snap the picture using the camera, the callback method will initiate the style transition:

```
findViewById(R.id.picture).setOnClickListener(new View.OnClickListener() {
    @Override
    public void onClick(View v) {
        captureStartTime = System.currentTimeMillis();
        mCameraView.captureImage(new
```

```
                    CameraKitEventCallback<CameraKitImage>() {
            @Override
            public void callback(CameraKitImage cameraKitImage) {
                byte[] jpeg = cameraKitImage.getJpeg();

                // Get the dimensions of the bitmap
                BitmapFactory.Options bmOptions = new
                                        BitmapFactory.Options();

                // Decode the image file into a Bitmap sized to fill
                //  the View
                //bmOptions.inJustDecodeBounds = false;
                  bmOptions.inMutable = true;

                long callbackTime = System.currentTimeMillis();
                Bitmap bitmap = BitmapFactory.decodeByteArray(jpeg, 0,
                            jpeg.length, bmOptions);
                ResultHolder.dispose();
                ResultHolder.setImage(bitmap);
    ResultHolder.setNativeCaptureSize(mCameraView.getCaptureSize());
                ResultHolder.setTimeToCallback(callbackTime -
                captureStartTime);
                Intent intent = new Intent(getApplicationContext(),
                                    ShowImageActivity.class);
                startActivity(intent);
            }
        });
    }
});
```

Alternatively, you have the option to pick an image from the mobile gallery using an intent:

```
mFile = new File(getExternalFilesDir(null), "pic.jpg");
Intent intent = new Intent();
intent.setType("image/*");
intent.setAction(Intent.ACTION_GET_CONTENT);
startActivityForResult(Intent.createChooser(intent, "Select Picture"),
            1);
```

The preceding code generates the following output:

You will get the results inside the onActivityResult method, demonstrated as follows:

```
@Override
public void onActivityResult(int requestCode, int resultCode, Intent data)
{
    super.onActivityResult(requestCode, resultCode, data);
    if (requestCode == 1 && resultCode == Activity.RESULT_OK) {
        if (data == null) {
            //Display an error
            return;
        }
        try {
```

```
            InputStream inputStream =
                    getContentResolver().openInputStream(data.getData());

            byte[] buffer = new byte[inputStream.available()];
            inputStream.read(buffer);

            // Get the dimensions of the bitmap
            BitmapFactory.Options bmOptions = new
                            BitmapFactory.Options();

            // Decode the image file into a Bitmap sized to fill the
            // View
            //bmOptions.inJustDecodeBounds = false;
            bmOptions.inMutable = true;

            Bitmap bitmap = BitmapFactory.decodeByteArray(buffer, 0,
                                        buffer.length, bmOptions);
            ResultHolder.dispose();
            ResultHolder.setImage(bitmap);
            Intent intent = new Intent(getApplicationContext(),
                                    ShowImageActivity.class);
            startActivity(intent);
        } catch (FileNotFoundException e) {
            e.printStackTrace();
        } catch (IOException e) {
            e.printStackTrace();
        }
        //Now you can do whatever you want with your inpustream, save
            it as file, upload to a server, decode a bitmap...
    }
    finish();
}
```

In .ShowImageActivity, a user interface resembling Instagram is built-in, and from this you can choose a variety of styles from the horizontal list at the bottom of our view and apply one to the selected picture. This is set up with a HorizontalListAdapter on a RecyclerView.

The thumbnail images for each style are loaded from the Assets folder as follows:

```
private void loadStyleBitmaps(){
    for(int i=0;i<NUM_STYLES;i++){
        try{
myStylesBmList.add(i,BitmapFactory.decodeStream(getAssets().open("thumb
                nails/style"+i+".jpg")));
        }
        catch(IOException e){
```

```
            e.printStackTrace();
            Toast.makeText(ShowImageActivity.this,"Alert! there is an
                issue while loading images",Toast.LENGTH_SHORT).show();
            finish();
        }
    }
}
```

The output of the preceding code is as follows:

To apply a style to the image when a particular style is picked, enter the following:

```
mRecyclerView.addOnItemTouchListener(new
    RecyclerItemClickListener(getApplicationContext(),mRecyclerView,new
    RecyclerItemClickListener.OnItemClickListener(){

    @Override
    public void onItemClick(View view, int position) {
        mSelectedStyle = position;
        progress = new ProgressDialog(ShowImageActivity.this);
        progress.setTitle("Loading");
        progress.setMessage("Applying your awesome style! Please
                        wait!");
        progress.setCancelable(false); // disable dismiss by tapping
                                        outside of the dialog
        progress.show();
        runInBackground(
                new Runnable() {
                    @Override
                    public void run() {
                        try {
                            stylizeImage();
                        }
                        catch(Exception e){
                            e.printStackTrace();
                            runOnUiThread(new Runnable() {
                                @Override
                                public void run() {
Toast.makeText(getApplicationContext(),"Oops! Some error
occurred!",Toast.LENGTH_SHORT).show();
                                    if(progress!=null){
                                        progress.dismiss();
                                    }
                                }
                            });
                        }
                    }
                });
    }

    @Override
    public void onLongItemClick(View view, int position) {
    }
}));
```

Then, call the styling method to apply the style:

```
private void stylizeImage() {
    if(bitmapCache.get("style_"+String.valueOf(mSelectedStyle))==null) {
        ActivityManager actManager = (ActivityManager)
getApplication().getSystemService(Context.ACTIVITY_SERVICE);
        ActivityManager.MemoryInfo memInfo = new
                                ActivityManager.MemoryInfo();
                                actManager.getMemoryInfo(memInfo);

        mImgBitmap = Bitmap.createBitmap(mOrigBitmap);
        for (int i = 0; i < NUM_STYLES; i++) {
            if (i == mSelectedStyle) {
                styleVals[i] = 1.0f;
            } else styleVals[i] = 0.0f;
        }
        mImgBitmap.getPixels(intValues, 0, mImgBitmap.getWidth(), 0, 0,
                    mImgBitmap.getWidth(), mImgBitmap.getHeight());

        for(int i=0;i<MY_DIVISOR;i++) {
            float[] floatValuesInput = new
float[floatValues.length/MY_DIVISOR];
            int myArrayLength = intValues.length/MY_DIVISOR;
            for(int x=0;x < myArrayLength;++x){
                final int myPos = x+i*myArrayLength;
                final int val = intValues[myPos];
                floatValuesInput[x * 3] = ((val >> 16) & 0xFF) /
                                                255.0f;
                floatValuesInput[x * 3 + 1] = ((val >> 8) & 0xFF) /
                                                255.0f;
                floatValuesInput[x * 3 + 2] = (val & 0xFF) / 255.0f;
            }
            Log.i(ShowImageActivity.class.getName(),"Sending following data
to tensorflow : floarValuesInput length : " + floatValuesInput.length+"
image bitmap height :" + mImgBitmap.getHeight() + " image bitmap width : "
+ mImgBitmap.getWidth());
            // Copy the input data into TensorFlow.
            inferenceInterface.feed(
                    INPUT_NODE, floatValuesInput, 1,
mImgBitmap.getHeight()/MY_DIVISOR, mImgBitmap.getWidth(), 3);
            inferenceInterface.feed(STYLE_NODE, styleVals, NUM_STYLES);
            inferenceInterface.run(new String[]{OUTPUT_NODE},
                                isDebug());
            float[] floatValuesOutput = new
float[floatValues.length/MY_DIVISOR];
            //floatValuesOutput  = new float[mImgBitmap.getWidth() *
(mImgBitmap.getHeight() + 10) * 3];//add a little buffer to the float array
because tensorflow sometimes returns larger images than what is given as
```

```
input
          inferenceInterface.fetch(OUTPUT_NODE, floatValuesOutput);

          for (int j = 0; j < myArrayLength; ++j) {
              intValues[j+i*myArrayLength] =
                      0xFF000000
                              | (((int) (floatValuesOutput [(j) * 3]
                                                    * 255)) << 16)
                              | (((int) (floatValuesOutput [(j) * 3 +
                                              1] * 255)) << 8)
                              | ((int) (floatValuesOutput [(j) * 3 +
                                              2] * 255));
          }
          //floatValues = new float[mImgBitmap.getWidth() *
                                  (mImgBitmap.getHeight()) * 3];
          mImgBitmap.setPixels(intValues, 0, mImgBitmap.getWidth(),
              0, 0, mImgBitmap.getWidth(), mImgBitmap.getHeight());
          runOnUiThread(new Runnable() {
              @Override
              public void run() {
                  mPreviewImage.setImageBitmap(mImgBitmap);
              }
          });
      }
  }
  else{
      mImgBitmap =
bitmapCache.get("style_"+String.valueOf(mSelectedStyle));
  }
  runOnUiThread(new Runnable() {
      @Override
      public void run() {
          if(mPreviewImage!=null){
              mPreviewImage.setImageBitmap(mImgBitmap);
bitmapCache.put("style_"+String.valueOf(mSelectedStyle),mImgBitmap);
              if(progress!=null){
                  progress.dismiss();
              }
          }
      }
  });
}
```

The output of the preceding code is as follows:

After applying the style, the image can be shared:

```
shareButton.setOnClickListener(new View.OnClickListener() {
    @Override
    public void onClick(View view) {
        if(ContextCompat.checkSelfPermission(ShowImageActivity.this,
                    Manifest.permission.WRITE_EXTERNAL_STORAGE)
            != PackageManager.PERMISSION_GRANTED)
        {
            requestStoragePermission();
            return;
        }
```

```
        if(mImgBitmap!=null) {
            try{
                Bitmap newBitmap =
Bitmap.createBitmap(mImgBitmap.getWidth(), mImgBitmap.getHeight(),
                                    Bitmap.Config.ARGB_8888);
                // create a canvas where we can draw on
                Canvas canvas = new Canvas(newBitmap);
                // create a paint instance with alpha
                canvas.drawBitmap(mOrigBitmap,0,0,null);
                Paint alphaPaint = new Paint();
                alphaPaint.setAlpha(mSeekBar.getProgress()*255/100);
                // now lets draw using alphaPaint instance
                canvas.drawBitmap(mImgBitmap, 0, 0, alphaPaint);

                String path =
MediaStore.Images.Media.insertImage(ShowImageActivity.this.getContentRe
solver(), newBitmap, "Title", null);
                final Intent intent = new
Intent(android.content.Intent.ACTION_SEND);
                intent.setFlags(Intent.FLAG_ACTIVITY_NEW_TASK);
                intent.putExtra(Intent.EXTRA_STREAM, Uri.parse(path));
                intent.setType("image/png");
                startActivity(intent);
            }
            catch(Exception e){
                e.printStackTrace();
                Toast.makeText(ShowImageActivity.this,"Error occurred while
trying to share",Toast.LENGTH_SHORT).show();
            }

        }
    }
});
```

We then need to get the appropriate permission from the user before performing any action on their data:

```
private void requestStoragePermission() {
    if
(ActivityCompat.shouldShowRequestPermissionRationale(ShowImageActivity.
        this, Manifest.permission.WRITE_EXTERNAL_STORAGE)) {
        Toast.makeText(ShowImageActivity.this,"Write permission required to
share",Toast.LENGTH_SHORT).show();
    }
    ActivityCompat.requestPermissions(this, new
String[]{Manifest.permission.WRITE_EXTERNAL_STORAGE},
        REQUEST_STORAGE_PERMISSION);
}
```

```
@Override
public void onRequestPermissionsResult(int requestCode, @NonNull String[]
permissions,
                                        @NonNull int[] grantResults) {
    if (requestCode == REQUEST_STORAGE_PERMISSION) {
        if (grantResults.length != 1 || grantResults[0] !=
PackageManager.PERMISSION_GRANTED) {
Camera2BasicFragment.ErrorDialog.newInstance(getString(R.string.request_per
mission_storage)).show(getFragmentManager(),"dialog");
        }
        else{
            shareButton.performClick();
        }
    } else {
        shareButton.performClick();
        super.onRequestPermissionsResult(requestCode, permissions,
grantResults);
    }
}
```

Summary

In this chapter, we learned to build a style transfer app from an art form. Now, we are very much familiar with how deep CNNs work and how layers process data. We have also become familiar with building the basic foundations of an iOS app and an Android app.

In the next chapter, we will discuss applying machine learning using Firebase's ML Kit framework in more detail.

References

- https://arxiv.org/abs/1508.06576
- https://harishnarayanan.org/writing/artistic-style-transfer/
- https://medium.com/tensorflow/neural-style-transfer-creating-art-with-deep-learning-using-tf-keras-and-eager-execution-7d541ac31398
- https://towardsdatascience.com/artistic-style-transfer-b7566a216431
- https://github.com/anishathalye/neural-style
- https://shafeentejani.github.io/2016-12-27/style-transfer/
- https://reiinakano.github.io/fast-style-transfer-deeplearnjs/
- https://arxiv.org/abs/1603.08155

Deep Diving into the ML Kit with Firebase

4

In this chapter, we are going to further explore the Google Firebase-based ML Kit platform for mobile applications.

Google launched Firebase ML Kit at I/O 2018. The ML Kit is a part of the Firebase application suite that enables developers to incorporate **machine learning** (**ML**) capabilities into mobile applications. The Firebase ML Kit **Software Development Kit** (**SDK**) comes with a few features that are common among mobile applications, helping Android and iOS developers irrespective of their familiarity with ML.

The concepts covered throughout the chapter are as follows:

- Understanding the basics of the ML Kit
- Learning to add Firebase to our applications
- Creating multiple applications that can be used for face detection, barcode scanning, and on-device text recognition using Firebase

Here is a link to our repository for this chapter: `https://github.com/intrepidkarthi/MLmobileapps/tree/master/Chapter4` and `https://github.com/PacktPublishing/Machine-Learning-Projects-for-Mobile-Applications`.

ML Kit basics

Of course, we can always do all the ML-based implementations without the help of Firebase. However, there are a few reasons why not everyone will be able to do this. The reason for this could be one of the following:

- A very good mobile application developer may not be good at building an ML model. Building an ML model definitely takes time. This may vary on a case-by-case basis.
- Finding the right set of data models that will solve your use case will be a very difficult problem. Let's say you want to detect age and gender classification on an Asian person's face. In this case, the existing models that are available may not be accurate enough for your use case.
- Hosting your own model will be costlier and will require extra care on the server side of the application.

The ML Kit is a combination of Google Cloud Vision API, Mobile Vision, and TensorFlow Lite models on a local device:

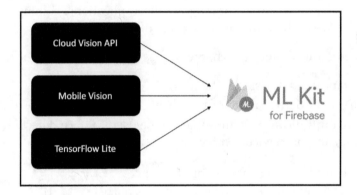

Basic feature set

ML Kit comes with a ready-to-use code base for common use cases such as detecting faces from an image, barcode scanning, finding text in an image, and image labeling. By passing on the data to the API, we can get the answer to our query on basic use cases with a few lines of code.

The ML Kit provides both on-device as well as cloud APIs. Based on our requirements, we can use either one of these services. While on-device APIs work faster, cloud APIs will provide better accuracy.

Not all mobile applications fall under the default APIs provided with the ML Kit. We will always have our own case to solve through ML. ML Kit supports deploying our custom TensorFlow Lite model into a cloud and acts as a layer to interact with your model.

At the time of writing this book, ML Kit comes with the following capabilities in beta mode:

- Text recognition
- Face detection
- Barcode scanning
- Image labeling
- Landmark detection

Depending on the use case, these capabilities can come with on-device and cloud-based detection. For example, detecting a face from an image while offline can be achieved on the device programmatically, rather than by uploading the image to the cloud and getting the results. At the same time, detecting a landmark from an image can't be done efficiently offline, since the data will vary from time to time and the amount of data on landmarks will be vast.

We will cover one basic example of every one of the aforementioned features in the Android application that we are going to build. Running the ML model in the cloud comes with two major concerns when developing the application:

- The applications need to use the internet. We generally apply ML on top of text, image, audio, and video. Based on our use case, we might end up spending more in data bandwidth.
- The application won't stay only with you. When the data from your device leaves your device, you may not have control of it.

Keeping these concerns in mind, we need to think of building a better ML-based application. The following table shows the availability of each API on the local device as well as in the cloud:

API	On-Cloud API	On-Device API
Text recognition	Yes	Yes
Face detection	No	Yes
Barcode scanning	No	Yes
Image labelling	Yes	Yes
Landmark detection	Yes	No
Custom TensorFlow Lite model	No	Yes

Building the application

We will now install a new Android application using Android Studio. To do this, install the latest Android Studio and create a new project, demonstrated as follows:

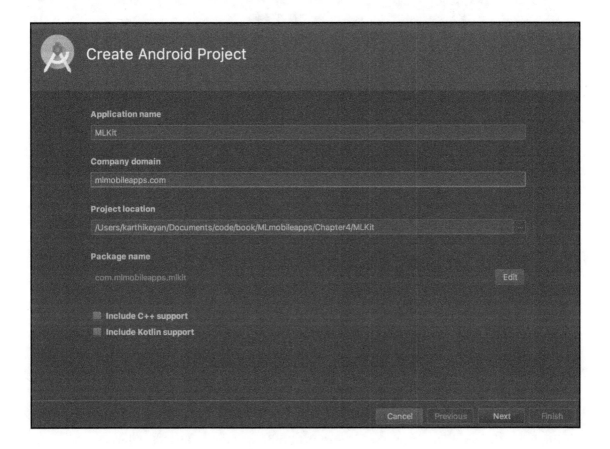

The next screenshot depicts which Android API we are going to target. Selecting **API 15** and above covers almost all existing Android devices, so it would be advisable to use that:

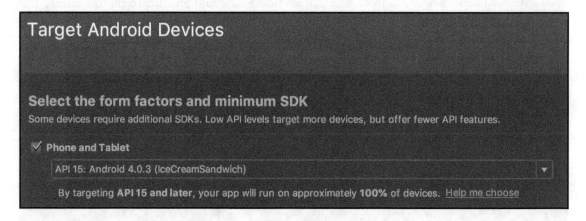

Adding Firebase to our application

We have created the Android Studio application with a blank activity in it. If you are using Android Studio 2.2 or any later versions, use the Firebase Assistant to connect your app to Firebase. The Assistant will help you to connect to an existing Firebase project or create a new one. It will also install all the necessary *Gradle dependencies*. In addition to this, we can manually add the Firebase project.

 This project is built using Android Studio Version 3.1.3.

If you don't find the Firebase Assistant under your **Tools** section, go to **File** | **Settings** | **Build, Execution and Deployment** | **Required Plugins** and add **Firebase Services**. Alternatively, you can manually add it by following these steps:

1. Go to `https://console.firebase.google.com/`. The following screenshot helps us understand what our page looks like:

The preceding screenshot shows how to add a new project. An alternative could be using an existing project from Firebase. This application supports projects across Android, iOS, and web platforms. After that, add more details about your app on the Firebase console. You can get your Android package name here from the `build.gradle` file under the application's `app` folder:

2. Download the `google-services.json` file.

   You can download the file from the Firebase control once the app has been created:

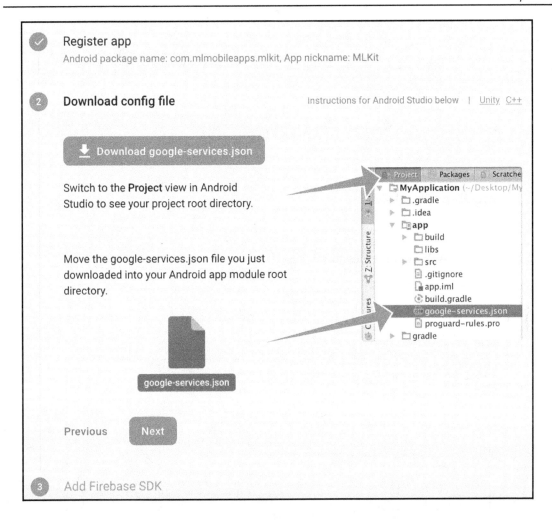

You can then place the `.json` file inside your application's `app` folder.

3. We then proceed to make changes to the `build.gradle` file. You will need to make changes at both project-level and app-level `build.gradle` files.

The project-level `build.gradle` file is placed under your project's main folder (`<project>/ build.gradle`):

```
buildscript {
    repositories {
        google()
        jcenter()
    }
```

```
    dependencies {
        classpath 'com.android.tools.build:gradle:3.1.3'
        classpath 'com.google.gms:google-services:4.0.0'
    }
}
```

The app-level `build.gradle` file is placed under the following folder: `<project>/<app-module>/build.gradle`. Add the following lines into it:

```
dependencies {
  // Add this line
  compile 'com.google.firebase:firebase-core:16.0.0'}
...
// Add to the bottom of the file
apply plugin: 'com.google.gms.google-services'
```

This includes the Analytics service of Firebase by default.

Now, click on the **Sync Now** button in the upper-right corner of the IDE.

Once this is done, run the application either on a connected Android device or on a simulator:

The message seen in the preceding screenshot confirms that the Firebase configuration has successfully been completed. You can now see that one user is added under the new application inside the console.

Now, let's jump into building features into our application. Before we begin, we need to add the ML Kit dependency in the app-level `build.gradle` file as follows:

```
dependencies {
  // You should always use the latest version
  implementation 'com.google.firebase:firebase-ml-vision:16.0.0'
}
```

In Firebase, you will be put on the Spark plan by default. You can upgrade to the Blaze plan in order to use Cloud Vision APIs, which has a monthly limit of 1,000 requests under the free plan. In this chapter, we will use all their on-device modules on a live camera feed.

With on-device training, the models will be downloaded automatically when we run the application for the first time. If we want to download only those specific models, this can be done by adding the following metadata to your application `manifest` file:

```
<application ...>
  ...
  <meta-data
      android:name="com.google.firebase.ml.vision.DEPENDENCIES"
      android:value="ocr" />
  <!-- To use multiple models: android:value="ocr, barcode, face, model4,
model5" -->
</application>
```

The use of a specific model depends on the application. If the ML model is going to be a core part of your application experience, this will make sense. Otherwise, the models should be downloaded only when they are required. This will reduce unnecessary load on the mobile device.

In the application that we are building, we are going to launch the camera view, from where we will switch into all the on-device ML provisions that we have with ML Kit.

At the bottom of the camera view, we will add a `spinner`, at which point we will pick the current ML functionality:

```
Spinner spinner = (Spinner) findViewById(R.id.spinner);
//Adding the list of items to be detected
List<String> options = new ArrayList<>();
options.add(FACE_DETECTION);
options.add(TEXT_DETECTION);
options.add(BARCODE_DETECTION);
options.add(IMAGE_LABEL_DETECTION);
options.add(CLASSIFICATION);
// Creating adapter for spinner
ArrayAdapter<String> dataAdapter = new ArrayAdapter<>(this,
                            R.layout.spinner_style, options);
// Drop down layout style - list view with radio button
dataAdapter.setDropDownViewResource(android.R.layout.simple_spinner_dro
                                    pdown_item);
// attaching data adapter to spinner
spinner.setAdapter(dataAdapter);
spinner.setOnItemSelectedListener(this);
```

Based on the user selection, the camera view will start showing results in the real-time camera view. Let's begin with face detection.

Face detection

With face detection, you can automatically detect human faces in an image or video. This reports the actual position of the face inside the media with size and orientation. Once a face is identified, we can further detect other body parts in it such as nose, eyes, and mouth. The face detection API detects the following:

- Bounding box of the detected face
- Tilt angle and rotating angle of the face
- Coordinates of the nose base, bottom of the mouth, left-hand side of the mouth, and right-hand side of the mouth
- Probability that the left eye is open, the right eye is open, and the person is smiling

There are a few terms associated with the face detection feature of ML Kit.

Face orientation tracking

Face tracking can be used to detect a particular face in a video. We can calculate the amount of frames that a particular face appears in, and we can also detect whether two faces are similar based on the position and motion of the face (this is typically possible in a video).

Face position is tracked using Euler angles, which identify the position of the face from the camera's angle:

- **Euler X**: A face with a positive Euler X angle is facing upward
- **Euler Y**: A face with a positive Euler Y angle is turned to the camera's right and to its left
- **Euler Z**: A face with a positive Euler Z angle is rotated counterclockwise relative to the camera

Among these three angles, ML Kit only supports the detection of the Euler Z angle; it doesn't support the Euler X angle, and the Euler Y angle is only measured when the camera is running in the *accurate* mode. With the *fast* mode, the camera makes shortcuts to bring results faster.

Landmarks

The ML Kit can detect **landmark** points that make up a face. These landmark points include the left eye, right eye, nose base, left-hand side of the mouth, and so on.

It detects the face independent of landmark information and doesn't use landmark information as the basis for identifying the whole face, so it is not enabled by default.

From the associated Euler Y angle, all the following landmarks can be identified:

	< -36 degrees	-36 to -12 degrees	-12 to 12 degrees	12 to 36 degrees	> 36 degrees
Left Eye	Yes	Yes	Yes	Yes	No
Right Eye	No	Yes	Yes	Yes	Yes
Left Mouth	Yes	Yes	Yes	No	No
Right Mouth	No	No	Yes	Yes	Yes
Bottom Mouth	No	Yes	Yes	Yes	No
Left Ear	Yes	Yes	No	No	No
Right Ear	No	No	No	Yes	Yes
Nose Base	Yes	Yes	Yes	Yes	Yes
Left Cheek	Yes	Yes	Yes	No	No
Right Cheek	No	No	Yes	Yes	Yes

Each detected landmark includes its associated position in the image. Here is how it is written in code:

```java
/** Draws the face annotations for position on the supplied canvas. */
@Override
public void draw(Canvas canvas) {
  FirebaseVisionFace face = firebaseVisionFace;
  if (face == null) {
    return;
  }

  // Draws a circle at the position of the detected face, with the
  // face's track id below.
  float x = translateX(face.getBoundingBox().centerX());
  float y = translateY(face.getBoundingBox().centerY());

  canvas.drawCircle(x, y, FACE_POSITION_RADIUS, facePositionPaint);
  canvas.drawText("id: " + face.getTrackingId(), x + ID_X_OFFSET, y +
                ID_Y_OFFSET, idPaint);

  canvas.drawText("happiness: " +
      String.format("%.2f", face.getSmilingProbability()),
      x + ID_X_OFFSET * 3,
      y - ID_Y_OFFSET,
      idPaint);
```

```
if (facing == CameraSource.CAMERA_FACING_FRONT) {
    canvas.drawText(
    "right eye: " + String.format("%.2f",
                        face.getRightEyeOpenProbability()),
                        x - ID_X_OFFSET,
                        y,
                        idPaint);
    canvas.drawText("left eye: " + String.format("%.2f",
                        face.getLeftEyeOpenProbability()),
                        x + ID_X_OFFSET * 6,
                        y,
                        idPaint);
}
else
{
    canvas.drawText(
        "left eye: " + String.format("%.2f",
                            face.getLeftEyeOpenProbability()),
                            x - ID_X_OFFSET, y, idPaint);
    canvas.drawText(
        "right eye: " + String.format("%.2f",
                            face.getRightEyeOpenProbability()),
                            x + ID_X_OFFSET * 6, y, idPaint);
}

// Draws a bounding box around the face.
float xOffset = scaleX(face.getBoundingBox().width() / 2.0f);
float yOffset = scaleY(face.getBoundingBox().height() / 2.0f);
float left = x - xOffset;
float top = y - yOffset;
float right = x + xOffset;
float bottom = y + yOffset;
canvas.drawRect(left, top, right, bottom, boxPaint);

// draw landmarks
drawLandmarkPosition(canvas, face,
                    FirebaseVisionFaceLandmark.BOTTOM_MOUTH);
drawLandmarkPosition(canvas, face,
                    FirebaseVisionFaceLandmark.LEFT_CHEEK);
drawLandmarkPosition(canvas, face,
                    FirebaseVisionFaceLandmark.LEFT_EAR);
drawLandmarkPosition(canvas, face,
                    FirebaseVisionFaceLandmark.LEFT_MOUTH);
drawLandmarkPosition(canvas, face,
                    FirebaseVisionFaceLandmark.LEFT_EYE);
drawLandmarkPosition(canvas, face,
                    FirebaseVisionFaceLandmark.NOSE_BASE);
drawLandmarkPosition(canvas, face,
```

```
                              FirebaseVisionFaceLandmark.RIGHT_CHEEK);
        drawLandmarkPosition(canvas, face,
                              FirebaseVisionFaceLandmark.RIGHT_EAR);
        drawLandmarkPosition(canvas, face,
                              FirebaseVisionFaceLandmark.RIGHT_EYE);
        drawLandmarkPosition(canvas, face,
                              FirebaseVisionFaceLandmark.RIGHT_MOUTH);
    }
```

With the preceding code, we can draw the facial landmark positions in a face along with a bounding box rectangle around the detected face.

Classification

Classification is used to classify images based on certain facial features, such as whether the eyes are open or closed and whether the person is smiling or not.

Classification is expressed as a value between 0 and 1. For example, a happiness value of 0.7 or more in the smiling classification can classify that the person is smiling. Similarly, the status of whether the eyes are open or not can be tracked through classification.

Both of these classifications rely on landmark detection. The *eyes open* and *smiling* classifications work on the frontal faces alone. This means that they need a smaller Euler Y angle (+/- 18 degrees) in order to calculate these factors.

Implementing face detection

Face detection needs this additional dependency to be added to the app-level `build.gradle` file:

```
    implementation 'com.google.firebase:firebase-ml-vision:16.0.0'
```

Face detector configuration

To initiate facial recognition, we need to create a `FirebaseVisionFaceDetectorOptions` instance. Let's create a new instance:

```
    FirebaseVisionFaceDetectorOptions options =
                            FirebaseVisionFaceDetectorOptions.Builder()
```

This can then be configured with a collection of different properties:

- **Detection mode**: Favors speed or accuracy when detecting faces. This can either be set to ACCURATE_MODE or FAST_MODE. This defaults to FAST_MODE:

```
.setModeType(FirebaseVisionFaceDetectorOptions.ACCURATE_MODE)
.setModeType(FirebaseVisionFaceDetectorOptions.FAST_MODE)
```

- **Landmark detection**: Determines whether or not to attempt to identify facial landmarks: eyes, ears, nose, cheeks, mouth. This defaults to NO_LANDMARKS:

```
.setLandmarkType(FirebaseVisionFaceDetectorOptions.ALL_LANDMARKS)
.setLandmarkType(FirebaseVisionFaceDetectorOptions.NO_LANDMARKS)
```

- **Feature classification**: Determines whether or not to classify faces into categories such as *smiling* and *eyes open*. This defaults to NO_CLASSIFICATIONS:

```
.setClassificationType(FirebaseVisionFaceDetectorOptions.ALL_
                                        CLASSIFICATIONS)
.setClassificationType(FirebaseVisionFaceDetectorOptions.NO_
                                        CLASSIFICATIONS)
```

- **Minimum face size**: This is the minimum size of faces to detect, relative to the image:

```
.setMinFaceSize(0.15f)
```

- **Enable face tracking**: Determines whether or not to assign faces an ID, which can be used to track faces across images:

```
.setTrackingEnabled(true)
.setTrackingEnabled(false)
```

By putting all of these together, we are left with the following:

```
val options = FirebaseVisionFaceDetectorOptions.Builder()
        .setModeType(FirebaseVisionFaceDetectorOptions.FAST_MODE)
        .setLandmarkType(
            FirebaseVisionFaceDetectorOptions.ALL_LANDMARKS)
        .setClassificationType(
            FirebaseVisionFaceDetectorOptions.ALL_CLASSIFICATIONS)
        .setMinFaceSize(0.20f)
        .setTrackingEnabled(true)
        .build()
```

If you don't set any of the options with the builder, then they will just be set to the default values that were stated previously.

Running the face detector

Let's look at the step-by-step process for running the face detector. Here is a diagram that shows a bounding box of a face along with all the facial landmark position marks:

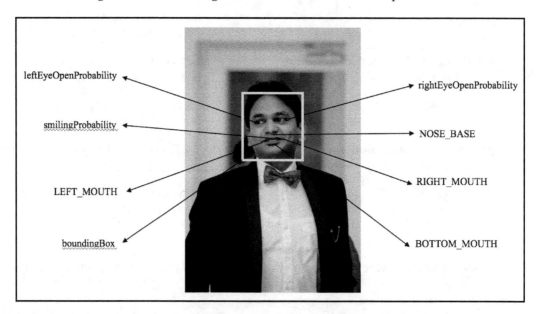

A bounding box is an area defined by two longitudes and two latitudes, where: latitude is a decimal number between -90.0 and 90.0 and longitude is a decimal number between -180.0 and 180.0.

Step one: creating a FirebaseVisionImage from the input

To run face detection, we need to create an instance of the `FirebaseVisionFace` class. There are five ways to create a `FirebaseVisionFace` object. The object can be created from either a bitmap, ByteBuffer, `media.Image`, ByteArray, or a file on the device.

Then, the created `FirebaseVisionImage` object will be passed on to the `FirebaseVisionFaceDetector` object's `detectInImage()` method.

Using a bitmap

Let's create this instance of a `FirebaseVisionImage` using an instance of a bitmap, where the object in the image should switch up right and no rotation is needed. We can create the instance by passing a bitmap into the `fromBitmap()` function; this will give us a `FirebaseVisionImage` as follows:

```
FirebaseVisionImage myImage = FirebaseVisionImage.fromBitmap(bitmap);
```

From media.Image

Let's create this instance of a `FirebaseVisionImage` using a `media.Image` instance. This may occur when capturing an image from the device's camera. When doing so, we must pass the instance of this image as well as the rotation of it, so this must be calculated prior to calling the `fromMediaImage()` function.

The rotation function is as follows:

```java
private static final SparseIntArray ORIENTATIONS = new
                                            SparseIntArray();
static {
    ORIENTATIONS.append(Surface.ROTATION_0, 90);
    ORIENTATIONS.append(Surface.ROTATION_90, 0);
    ORIENTATIONS.append(Surface.ROTATION_180, 270);
    ORIENTATIONS.append(Surface.ROTATION_270, 180);
}

/**
 * Get the angle by which an image must be rotated given the device's
   current orientation.
 */
@RequiresApi(api = Build.VERSION_CODES.LOLLIPOP)
private int getRotationCompensation(String cameraId, Activity activity,
                                Context context)
      throws CameraAccessException {
    // Get the device's current rotation relative to its "native"
    // orientation.
    // Then, from the ORIENTATIONS table, look up the angle the image
    // must be rotated to compensate for the device's rotation.
    int deviceRotation =
        activity.getWindowManager().getDefaultDisplay().getRotation();
        int rotationCompensation = ORIENTATIONS.get(deviceRotation);
```

```
    // On most devices, the sensor orientation is 90 degrees, but for some
    // devices it is 270 degrees. For devices with a sensor orientation of
    // 270, rotate the image an additional 180 ((270 + 270) % 360) degrees.
        CameraManager cameraManager = (CameraManager)
    context.getSystemService(CAMERA_SERVICE);
        int sensorOrientation = cameraManager
                .getCameraCharacteristics(cameraId)
                .get(CameraCharacteristics.SENSOR_ORIENTATION);
        rotationCompensation = (rotationCompensation + sensorOrientation +
                            270) % 360;

    // Return the corresponding FirebaseVisionImageMetadata rotation value.
        int result;
        switch (rotationCompensation) {
            case 0:
                result = FirebaseVisionImageMetadata.ROTATION_0;
                break;
            case 90:
                result = FirebaseVisionImageMetadata.ROTATION_90;
                break;
            case 180:
                result = FirebaseVisionImageMetadata.ROTATION_180;
                break;
            case 270:
                result = FirebaseVisionImageMetadata.ROTATION_270;
                break;
            default:
                result = FirebaseVisionImageMetadata.ROTATION_0;
                Log.e(TAG, "Bad rotation value: " + rotationCompensation);
        }
        return result;
    }
```

The result will then be passed on to the method as follows:

```
FirebaseVisionImage myImage =
            FirebaseVisionImage.fromMediaImage(mediaImage, rotation);
```

From a ByteBuffer

Let's create this instance of a `FirebaseVisionImage` using a ByteBuffer. To do so, though, we must first create an instance of a `FirebaseVisionImageMetadata`. This contains the data required to construct the vision image, such as format, rotation, and measurements (height and width) as follows:

```
FirebaseVisionImageMetadata metadata = new
    FirebaseVisionImageMetadata.Builder()
```

```
.setWidth(1280)
.setHeight(720)
.setFormat(FirebaseVisionImageMetadata.IMAGE_FORMAT_NV21)
.setRotation(rotation)
.build();
```

We can then pass this along with our ByteBuffer to create the following instance:

```
FirebaseVisionImage myImage =
            FirebaseVisionImage.fromByteBuffer(buffer, metadata);
```

From a ByteArray

Creating an image from a ByteArray works in the same way as a ByteBuffer, except we must use the `fromByteArray()` function instead:

```
FirebaseVisionImage myImage =
            FirebaseVisionImage.fromByteArray(byteArray, metadata);
```

From a file

A vision image instance can be created from a file by calling the `fromFilePath()` function with a context and the desired **Uniform Resource Identifier (URI)**:

```
val image: FirebaseVisionImage?
try {
    image = FirebaseVisionImage.fromFilePath(context, uri);
} catch (IOException e) {
    e.printStackTrace();
}
```

Step two: creating an instance of FirebaseVisionFaceDetector object

`FirebaseVisionFaceDetector` detects `<FirebaseVisionFace>` instances in the input image. After running the face detector, create an instance of `FirebaseVisionFaceDetector` as follows:

```
FirebaseVisionFaceDetector detector = FirebaseVision.getInstance()
.getVisionFaceDetector(options);
```

The preceding method returns a task that asynchronously returns a list of detected FirebaseVisionFaces (Task<List<FirebaseVisionFace>>). The created object will then be passed on to the image detection method.

 Always remember to check the console for errors generated by the constructor.

Step three: image detection

Based on the image detection, the listener callback will come into either success or failure methods. The output will contain the list of identified faces with bounding boxes.

Finally, pass the image to the detectInImage() method as follows:

```
@Override
protected Task<List<FirebaseVisionFace>> detectInImage(FirebaseVisionImage
image) {
   return detector.detectInImage(image);
}

@Override
protected void onSuccess(
    @NonNull List<FirebaseVisionFace> faces,
    @NonNull FrameMetadata frameMetadata,
    @NonNull GraphicOverlay graphicOverlay) {
   graphicOverlay.clear();
   for (int i = 0; i < faces.size(); ++i) {
     FirebaseVisionFace face = faces.get(i);
     FaceGraphic faceGraphic = new FaceGraphic(graphicOverlay);
     graphicOverlay.add(faceGraphic);
     faceGraphic.updateFace(face, frameMetadata.getCameraFacing());
   }
}

@Override
protected void onFailure(@NonNull Exception e) {
   Log.e(TAG, "Face detection failed " + e);
}
```

Retrieving information from detected faces

If the face recognition operation succeeds, a list of `FirebaseVisionFace` objects will be passed to the successful listener. Each `FirebaseVisionFace` object represents a face that was detected in the image. For each face, you can get its bounding coordinates in the input image, as well as any other information you configured the face detector to find:

```
for (FirebaseVisionFace face : faces) {
    Rect bounds = face.getBoundingBox();
    float rotY = face.getHeadEulerAngleY();   // Head is rotated to the
                                              // right rotY degrees
    float rotZ = face.getHeadEulerAngleZ();   // Head is tilted sideways
                                              // rotZ degrees

    // If landmark detection was enabled (mouth, ears, eyes, cheeks, and
    // nose available):
    FirebaseVisionFaceLandmark leftEar =
            face.getLandmark(FirebaseVisionFaceLandmark.LEFT_EAR);
    if (leftEar != null) {
        FirebaseVisionPoint leftEarPos = leftEar.getPosition();
    }

    // If classification was enabled:
    if (face.getSmilingProbability() !=
            FirebaseVisionFace.UNCOMPUTED_PROBABILITY) {
        float smileProb = face.getSmilingProbability();
    }
    if (face.getRightEyeOpenProbability() !=
        FirebaseVisionFace.UNCOMPUTED_PROBABILITY) {
            float rightEyeOpenProb = face.getRightEyeOpenProbability();
    }

    // If face tracking was enabled:
    if (face.getTrackingId() != FirebaseVisionFace.INVALID_ID) {
        int id = face.getTrackingId();
    }
}
```

With this, we should be able to work on the face detector with ML Kit. Now, go to our repository to pull the code directly from there:

Here is a link to our repository for this chapter: `https://github.com/intrepidkarthi/MLmobileapps/tree/mast er/Chapter4`. and `https://github.com/PacktPublishing/Machine-Learning-Projects-for-Mobile-Applications`.

Barcode scanner

Let's now jump into implementing a mobile-based barcode scanner using ML Kit. There are many formats for barcodes. ML Kit supports all the following listed formats:

Once the barcode is identified on the camera view, the `draw` method puts the bounding box on top of it, along with the detected barcode's raw value. The following code draws the barcode block annotations for position, size, and raw value on the supplied `canvas`:

```
/**
 * Draws the barcode block annotations
 */
@Override
public void draw(Canvas canvas) {
  if (barcode == null) {
    throw new IllegalStateException("Attempting to draw a null
                                    barcode.");
  }

  // Draws the bounding box around the BarcodeBlock.
  RectF rect = new RectF(barcode.getBoundingBox());
  rect.left = translateX(rect.left);
  rect.top = translateY(rect.top);
  rect.right = translateX(rect.right);
  rect.bottom = translateY(rect.bottom);
  canvas.drawRect(rect, rectPaint);
```

```
    // Renders the barcode at the bottom of the box.
    canvas.drawText(barcode.getRawValue(), rect.left, rect.bottom,
                barcodePaint);
}
```

If we know the barcode format that we are about to read, we can speed up the process by detecting that format only while configuring the setup. For example, to detect QR codes, let's create the `FirebaseVisionBarcodeDetectorOptions` instance by setting the barcode format shown as follows:

```
FirebaseVisionBarcodeDetectorOptions options =
        new FirebaseVisionBarcodeDetectorOptions.Builder()
        .setBarcodeFormats(FirebaseVisionBarcode.FORMAT_QR_CODE)
        .build();
```

Now that we have defined this option, we can use the `get` function of our `FirebaseVision` instance, passing in our `options` instance:

```
val detector =
        FirebaseVision.getInstance().getVisionBarcodeDetector(options)
```

Step one: creating a FirebaseVisionImage object

After the options are built, we can go ahead with recognition. Similar to what we did with face detection, the `FirebaseVisionImage` object can be created from either a bitmap, ByteBuffer, `media.Image`, ByteArray, or file on the device.

From bitmap

Let's create this instance of a `FirebaseVisionImage` using a bitmap. To begin, let's pass a bitmap into the `fromBitmap()` method, which will give us back a `FirebaseVisionImage`:

```
FirebaseVisionImage image = FirebaseVisionImage.fromBitmap(bitmap);
```

From media.Image

Let's create this instance of a `FirebaseVisionImage` using a `media.Image` instance. This will be captured using the device camera. After the image is captured, we need to pass it on to the `rotation` method as well. `rotation` must be called before calling the `fromMediaImage()` method. The following method gets the angle by which an image must be rotated given the device's current orientation:

```java
@RequiresApi(api = Build.VERSION_CODES.LOLLIPOP)
private int getRotationCompensation(String cameraId, Activity activity,
                                    Context context)
        throws CameraAccessException {
// Get the device's current rotation relative to its "native"
   orientation.
// Then, from the ORIENTATIONS table, look up the angle the image must be
// rotated to compensate for the device's rotation.
    int deviceRotation =
        activity.getWindowManager().getDefaultDisplay().getRotation();
    int rotationCompensation = ORIENTATIONS.get(deviceRotation);

 // On most devices, the sensor orientation is 90 degrees, but for some
 // devices it is 270 degrees. For devices with a sensor orientation of
 // 270, rotate the image an additional 180 ((270 + 270) % 360)
    degrees.
    CameraManager cameraManager = (CameraManager)
context.getSystemService(CAMERA_SERVICE);
    int sensorOrientation = cameraManager
            .getCameraCharacteristics(cameraId)
            .get(CameraCharacteristics.SENSOR_ORIENTATION);
    rotationCompensation = (rotationCompensation + sensorOrientation +
                        270) % 360;

// Return the corresponding FirebaseVisionImageMetadata rotation value.
    int result;
    switch (rotationCompensation) {
        case 0:
            result = FirebaseVisionImageMetadata.ROTATION_0;
            break;
        case 90:
            result = FirebaseVisionImageMetadata.ROTATION_90;
            break;
        case 180:
            result = FirebaseVisionImageMetadata.ROTATION_180;
            break;
        case 270:
            result = FirebaseVisionImageMetadata.ROTATION_270;
            break;
```

```
        default:
            result = FirebaseVisionImageMetadata.ROTATION_0;
            Log.e(TAG, "Bad rotation value: " + rotationCompensation);
    }
    return result;
}
```

The previous method is the same as the one we used with face detection:

```
FirebaseVisionImage image =
        FirebaseVisionImage.fromMediaImage(mediaImage, rotation);
```

From ByteBuffer

Let's create this instance of a `FirebaseVisionImage` using a ByteBuffer. However, in order to do this, we must first create an instance of a `FirebaseVisionImageMetadata`. This contains the data required to construct the vision image, such as the rotation and measurements mentioned as follows:

```
FirebaseVisionImageMetadata metadata = new
    FirebaseVisionImageMetadata.Builder()
        .setWidth(1280)
        .setHeight(720)
        .setFormat(FirebaseVisionImageMetadata.IMAGE_FORMAT_NV21)
        .setRotation(rotation)
        .build();
```

With the preceding instance, we have the width and height of the input image. It can be configured according to your application's requirement.

 If you want to learn more about image format parameters, check out: https://developer.android.com/reference/android/graphics/ImageFormat.

We can then pass this along with our ByteBuffer to create the following instance:

```
FirebaseVisionImage image = FirebaseVisionImage.fromByteBuffer(buffer,
                            metadata);
```

From ByteArray

A ByteBuffer is like a builder to create a `byte[]`. Unlike arrays, it has more helper methods. Creating an image from a ByteArray works in the same way as a ByteBuffer, except we must use the `fromByteArray()` function instead shown as follows:

```
FirebaseVisionImage image =
            FirebaseVisionImage.fromByteArray(byteArray, metadata);
```

From file

A vision image instance can be created from a file by calling the `fromFilePath()` function with the context and URI:

```
val image: FirebaseVisionImage?
try {
    image = FirebaseVisionImage.fromFilePath(context, uri);
} catch (IOException e) {
    e.printStackTrace();
}
```

Step two: creating a FirebaseVisionBarcodeDetector object

`FirebaseVisionBarcodeDetector` recognizes barcodes (in a variety of one-dimensional and two-dimensional formats) in a supplied `FirebaseVisionImage` as follows:

```
FirebaseVisionBarcodeDetector detector =
FirebaseVision.getInstance().getVisionBarcodeDetector();
// Or, we can specify the formats to recognize:
FirebaseVisionBarcodeDetector detector =
FirebaseVision.getInstance().getVisionBarcodeDetector(options);
```

Step three: barcode detection

Based on the image detection, the listener callback will come into either success or failure methods. The output will contain the list of identified `FirebaseVisionBarcode` objects as follows:

```
@Override
protected Task<List<FirebaseVisionBarcode>>
```

```
detectInImage(FirebaseVisionImage image) {
    return detector.detectInImage(image);
}

@Override
protected void onSuccess(
        @NonNull List<FirebaseVisionBarcode> barcodes,
        @NonNull FrameMetadata frameMetadata,
        @NonNull GraphicOverlay graphicOverlay) {
    graphicOverlay.clear();
    for (int i = 0; i < barcodes.size(); ++i) {
        FirebaseVisionBarcode barcode = barcodes.get(i);
        BarcodeGraphic barcodeGraphic = new BarcodeGraphic(graphicOverlay,
barcode);
        graphicOverlay.add(barcodeGraphic);
    }
}

@Override
protected void onFailure(@NonNull Exception e) {
    Log.e(TAG, "Barcode detection failed " + e);
}
```

Upon successful detection of one or more barcodes, the `FirebaseVisionBarcode` objects need to be passed on to the methods in order to get data from the detected barcodes. Based on the type of barcode, we get the corresponding output as follows:

```
for (FirebaseVisionBarcode barcode: barcodes) {
    //Returns a Rect instance that contains the bounding box for the
recognized barcode
    Rect bounds = barcode.getBoundingBox();
//Returns the coordinates for each corner of the barcode.
    Point[] corners = barcode.getCornerPoints();
//Returns the barcode value in its raw format
    String rawValue = barcode.getRawValue();
//Returns the format type of the barcode
    int valueType = barcode.getValueType();
// See API reference for complete list of supported types
    switch (valueType) {
        case FirebaseVisionBarcode.TYPE_WIFI:
            String ssid = barcode.getWifi().getSsid();
            String password = barcode.getWifi().getPassword();
            int type = barcode.getWifi().getEncryptionType();
            break;
        case FirebaseVisionBarcode.TYPE_URL:
            String title = barcode.getUrl().getTitle();
            String url = barcode.getUrl().getUrl();
            break;
```

```
        }
    }
```

With this, we should now be able to work on barcode scanning with ML Kit. This will be a handy tool for any retail commerce applications:

Now, let's go to our repository to pull the code from there and start your experiment.

 Here is a link to our repository for
this chapter: `https://github.com/intrepidkarthi/MLmobileapps/tree/`
`master/Chapter4.` and `https://github.com/PacktPublishing/Machine-`
`Learning-Projects-for-Mobile-Applications`.

Text recognition

After face detection and barcode scanning, let's build an application to recognize text from the input images or camera feed. This method is called **Optical Character Recognition** (**OCR**). Text recognition supports both on-device recognition as well as cloud-based recognition.

On-device text recognition

Let's skip the default methods that we use for face detection and barcode scanning.

After creating the `FirebaseVisionImage` object, we will create the `detector` instance where we will pass on the `VisionImage` object shown as follows, similar to what we have done before on face detection and barcode scanning:

```
FirebaseVisionTextDetector detector = FirebaseVision.getInstance()
        .getVisionTextDetector();
```

Detecting text on a device

For text detection, pass the image object to the `detectInImage()` method from the `detector` instance. The following code block is used to do this:

```
Task<FirebaseVisionText> result =
        detector.detectInImage(image)
                .addOnSuccessListener(new
OnSuccessListener<FirebaseVisionText>() {
                    @Override
                    public void onSuccess(FirebaseVisionText
firebaseVisionText) {
                        // Task completed successfully
                        // ...
                    }
                })
                .addOnFailureListener(
                        new OnFailureListener() {
                            @Override
                            public void onFailure(@NonNull Exception e) {
                                // Task failed with an exception
                                // ...
                            }
                        });
```

Upon successful identification of text, we can parse the `FirebaseVisionText` object to process it further, using the following code block:

```
for (FirebaseVisionText.Block block: firebaseVisionText.getBlocks()) {
    Rect boundingBox = block.getBoundingBox();
    Point[] cornerPoints = block.getCornerPoints();
    String text = block.getText();

    for (FirebaseVisionText.Line line: block.getLines()) {
        // ...
        for (FirebaseVisionText.Element element: line.getElements()) {
            // ...
        }
    }
}
```

Now that we are comfortable with finding faces, barcodes, and text in any given media, let's look at an example of how to do text recognition in the cloud:

Cloud-based text recognition

To use cloud-based detection, we need to enable the Google Vision API on the developer console for your project. Cloud APIs come with an additional cost, but the first 1,000 calls to the API per month are free. Regardless, you still need to enter your credit card information to secure the subscription plan. Choose this in accordance with your needs.

Configuring the detector

We need to configure the `FirebaseVisionCloudDetectorOptions` object. By default, the cloud detector uses the `STABLE` version of this model and returns up to ten results. However, we can change this based on our needs and set the parameters as follows:

```
FirebaseVisionCloudDetectorOptions options =
  new FirebaseVisionCloudDetectorOptions.Builder()
  .setModelType(FirebaseVisionCloudDetectorOptions.LATEST_MODEL)
  .setMaxResults(12)
  .build();
```

To use the default settings, we can use `FirebaseVisionCloudDetectorOptions.DEFAULT` in the next step.

After this, we create the `FirebaseVisionImage` object. Since this was discussed in the previous implementation of a face detector and a barcode scanner, we will skip this part here.

Create a `detector` instance to pass on the image object:

```
FirebaseVisionCloudTextDetector detector = FirebaseVision.getInstance()
        .getVisionCloudTextDetector();
// Or, to change the default settings:
// FirebaseVisionCloudTextDetector detector = FirebaseVision.getInstance()
//        .getVisionCloudTextDetector(options);
```

Now, we can pass on the image object to the `detectInImage()` method:

```
Task<FirebaseVisionCloudText> result = detector.detectInImage(image)
        .addOnSuccessListener(new
OnSuccessListener<FirebaseVisionCloudText>() {
        @Override
        public void onSuccess(FirebaseVisionCloudText
firebaseVisionCloudText) {
            // Task completed successfully
            // ...
        }
```

```
    })
    .addOnFailureListener(new OnFailureListener() {
        @Override
        public void onFailure(@NonNull Exception e) {
            // Task failed with an exception
            // ...
        }
    });
```

Upon successful detection of text, we will get a list of text blocks. We can then process the outputs in order to proceed further as follows:

```
String recognizedText = firebaseVisionCloudText.getText();

for (FirebaseVisionCloudText.Page page: firebaseVisionCloudText.getPages())
{
    List<FirebaseVisionCloudText.DetectedLanguage> languages =
            page.getTextProperty().getDetectedLanguages();
    int height = page.getHeight();
    int width = page.getWidth();
    float confidence = page.getConfidence();

    for (FirebaseVisionCloudText.Block block: page.getBlocks()) {
        Rect boundingBox = block.getBoundingBox();
        List<FirebaseVisionCloudText.DetectedLanguage> blockLanguages =
                block.getTextProperty().getDetectedLanguages();
        float blockConfidence = block.getConfidence();
        // And so on: Paragraph, Word, Symbol
    }
}
```

Summary

At this point, we are quite comfortable with implementing the basic functionalities of a mobile-based ML application that involves in-text detection, face detection, and barcode scanning. Similarly, we can implement image labeling and landmark detection through the cloud API. We should now be able to see that ML Kit covers the basic needs of a mobile-based ML application.

In the next chapter, we shall move on to building the **Augmented Reality (AR)** filter similar to the ones available on Snapchat.

A Snapchat-Like AR Filter on Android

5

In this chapter, we will build an **Augmented Reality** (**AR**) filter that is used on applications such as Snapchat and Instagram using TensorFlow Lite. With this application, we will place AR filters on top of a real-time camera view. For example, we can add a mustache to a male's facial key point, and we can add a relevant emotional expression on top of the eyes. The TensorFlow Lite model is used to detect gender and emotion from the camera view.

In this chapter, we will understand the following concepts:

- MobileNet models
- Building the dataset required for model conversion
- Building the Android application

MobileNet models

We use the MobileNet model to identify gender, while the AffectNet model is used to detect emotion. Facial key point detection is achieved using Google's Mobile Vision API.

Neural networks and deep learning have sparked tremendous progress in the field of **natural language processing** (**NLP**) and computer vision. While many of the face, object, landmark, logo and text recognition technologies are provided for internet-connected devices, we believe that the ever-increasing computational power of mobile devices can enable the delivery of these technologies into the hands of users, anytime, anywhere, regardless of internet connection. However, computer vision for on device and embedded applications face many challenges—models must run quickly with high accuracy in a resource-constrained environment making use of limited computation, power, and space.

TensorFlow offers various pre-trained models, such as drag and drop models, in order to identify approximately 1,000 default objects. When compared with other similar models such as the Inception model datasets, MobileNet works better with latency, size, and accuracy. In terms of output performance, there is a significant amount of lag, with a full-fledged model. However, the trade-off is acceptable when the model is deployable on a mobile device and for real-time offline model detection.

You can refer to the code for this chapter at `https://github.com/intrepidkarthi/MLmobileapps/tree/master/Chapter5/ARfilter` and `https://github.com/PacktPublishing/Machine-Learning-Projects-for-Mobile-Applications`.

The MobileNet architecture deals with a 3 x 3 convolution layer in a different way from a typical CNN.

For a more detailed explanation of the MobileNet architecture, please visit `https://arxiv.org/pdf/1704.04861.pdf`.

Let's look at an example of how to use MobileNet. Let's not build one more generic dataset in this case. Instead, we will write a simple classifier to find Pikachu in an image. The following are sample pictures showing an image of Pikachu and an image without Pikachu:

Building the dataset

To build our own classifier, we need to have datasets that contain images with and without Pikachu. You can start with 1,000 images on each database and you can pull down such images here: `https://search.creativecommons.org/`.

Let's create two folders named `pikachu` and `no-pikachu` and drop those images accordingly. Always ensure that you have the appropriate licenses to use any images, especially for commercial purposes.

Image scrapper from the Google and Bing
API: `https://github.com/rushilsrivastava/image_search`.

Now we have an image folder, which is structured as follows:

```
/dataset/
      /pikachu/[image1,..]
      /no-pikachu/[image1,..]
```

Retraining of images

We can now start labeling our images. With TensorFlow, this job becomes easier. Assuming that you have installed TensorFlow already, download the following retraining script:

```
curl
 https://github.com/tensorflow/hub/blob/master/examples/
 image_retraining/retrain.py
```

Lets retrain the image with the Python script now:

```
python retrain.py \
  --image_dir ~/MLmobileapps/Chapter5/dataset/ \
  --learning_rate=0.0001 \
  --testing_percentage=20 \
  --validation_percentage=20 \
  --train_batch_size=32 \
  --validation_batch_size=-1 \
  --eval_step_interval=100 \
  --how_many_training_steps=1000 \
  --flip_left_right=True \
  --random_scale=30 \
  --random_brightness=30 \
  --architecture mobilenet_1.0_224 \
  --output_graph=output_graph.pb \
  --output_labels=output_labels.txt
```

 If you set `validation_batch_size` to −1, it will validate the whole dataset; `learning_rate = 0.0001` works well. You can adjust and try this for yourself. In the `architecture` flag, we choose which version of MobileNet to use, from versions 1.0, 0.75, 0.50, and 0.25. The suffix number `224` represents the image resolution. You can specify 224, 192, 160, or 128 as well.

Model conversion from GraphDef to TFLite

`TocoConverter` is used to convert from a TensorFlow `GraphDef` file or SavedModel into either a TFLite FlatBuffer or graph visualization. TOCO stands for *TensorFlow Lite Optimizing Converter*.

We need to pass the data through command-line arguments. There are a few command-line arguments listed in the following with `TensorFlow 1.10.0`:

```
--output_file OUTPUT_FILE
Filepath of the output tflite model.
--graph_def_file GRAPH_DEF_FILE
Filepath of input TensorFlow GraphDef.
--saved_model_dir
Filepath of directory containing the SavedModel.
--keras_model_file
Filepath of HDF5 file containing tf.Keras model.
--output_format {TFLITE,GRAPHVIZ_DOT}
Output file format.
--inference_type {FLOAT,QUANTIZED_UINT8}
Target data type in the output
--inference_input_type {FLOAT,QUANTIZED_UINT8}
Target data type of real-number input arrays.
--input_arrays INPUT_ARRAYS
Names of the input arrays, comma-separated.
--input_shapes INPUT_SHAPES
Shapes corresponding to --input_arrays, colon-separated.
--output_arrays OUTPUT_ARRAYS
Names of the output arrays, comma-separated.
```

We can now use the `toco` tool to convert the TensorFlow model into a TensorFlow Lite model:

```
toco \
  --graph_def_file=/tmp/output_graph.pb
  --output_file=/tmp/optimized_graph.tflite
  --input_arrays=Mul
  --output_arrays=final_result
  --input_format=TENSORFLOW_GRAPHDEF
  --output_format=TFLITE
  --input_shape=1,${224},${224},3
  --inference_type=FLOAT
  --input_data_type=FLOAT
```

Similarly, we have two model files used in this application: gender model and emotion model. These will be explained in the following two sections.

To convert ML models in TensorFlow 1.9.0 to TensorFlow 1.11.0, use TocoConverter. TocoConverter is semantically identically to TFLite Converter. To convert models prior to TensorFlow 1.9, use the `toco_convert` function. Run `help(tf.contrib.lite.toco_convert)` to get details about acceptable parameters.

Gender model

This is built on the `IMDB WIKI` dataset, which contains 500k+ celebrity faces. It uses the MobileNet_V1_224_0.5 version of MobileNet.

The link to the data model project can be found here: `https://data. vision.ee.ethz.ch/cvl/rrothe/imdb-wiki/`.

It is very rare to find public datasets with thousands of images. This dataset is built on top of a large collection of celebrity faces. There are two common places: one is IMDb and the other one is Wikipedia. More than 100K celebrities' details were retrieved from their profiles from both sources through scripts. Then it was organized by removing noises(irrelevant content). All the images without a timestamp were removed, assuming that images with a single photo are likely to show the person and the birth date details are correct. At the end, there were 460,723 faces from 20,284 celebrities from IMDb and 62,328 from Wikipedia, which totals 523,051.

The paper behind the model can be found here: `https://www.vision.ee. ethz.ch/en/publications/papers/proceedings/eth_biwi_01229.pdf`. The model says that it can be used only for research purpose. Though we could have reused the model from our chapter 2, we wanted to give you hands on with different model datasets, hence we picked this dataset of popular faces. You can choose your own model dataset based on the problem you solve and which is more suitable for you.

Author credits: @article{Rothe-IJCV-2016, author = {Rasmus Rothe and Radu Timofte and Luc Van Gool}, title = {Deep expectation of real and apparent age from a single image without facial landmarks}, journal = {International Journal of Computer Vision (IJCV)}, year = {2016}, month = {July}, }

Emotion model

This is built on the AffectNet model with more than 1 million images. It uses the MobileNet_V2_224_1.4 version of MobileNet.

The link to the data model project can be found here: `http://mohammadmahoor.com/affectnet/`.

The AffectNet model is built by collecting and annotating facial images of more than 1 million faces from the internet. The images were sourced from three search engines, using around 1,250 related keywords in six different languages. Among the collected images, half of the images were manually annotated for the presence of seven discrete facial expressions (categorical model) and the intensity of valence and arousal (dimensional model).

Comparison of MobileNet versions

In both of our models, we use different versions of MobileNet models. MobileNet V2 is mostly a updated version of V1 that makes it even more efficient and powerful in terms of performance. We will see a few factor between both the models:

Version	MACs(millions)	Parameters(millions)
MobileNet V1	569	4.24
MobileNet V2	300	3.47

The picture above shows the numbers from MobileNet V1 and V2 belong to the model versions with 1.0 depth multiplier. It is better, if the numbers are lower in this table. By seeing the results we can assume that V2 is almost twice as fast as V1 model. On a mobile device when memory access is limited than the computational capability V2 works very well.

MACs—multiply-accumulate operations. This measures how many calculations are needed to perform inference on a single 224×224 RGB image. When the image size increases more MACs are required.

From the number of MACs alone, V2 should be almost twice as fast as V1. However, it's not just about the number of calculations. On mobile devices, memory access is much slower than computation. But here V2 has the advantage too: it only has 80% of the parameter count that V1 has. Now lets look into the performance in terms of accuracy:

Version	Top 1 accuracy	Top 5 accuracy
MobileNet V1	70.9	89.9
MobileNet V2	71.8	91.0

The figure shown above are tested on ImageNet dataset. These numbers can be misleading as it depends on all the constraints that is taken into account while deriving these numbers.

The IEEE paper behind the model can be found here: `http://mohammadmahoor.com/wp-content/uploads/2017/08/AffectNet_oneColumn-2.pdf`.

Building the Android application

Now create a new Android project from Android Studio. This should be called `ARFilter`, or whatever name you prefer:

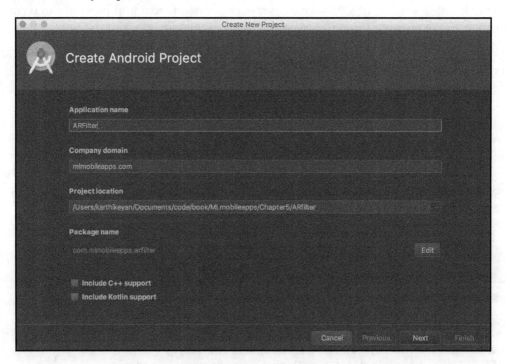

On the next screen, select the Android OS versions that our application supports and select **API 15** which is not shown on the image. That covers almost all existing Android phones. When you are ready, press **Next**. On the next screen, select **Add No Activity** and click Finish. This creates an empty project:

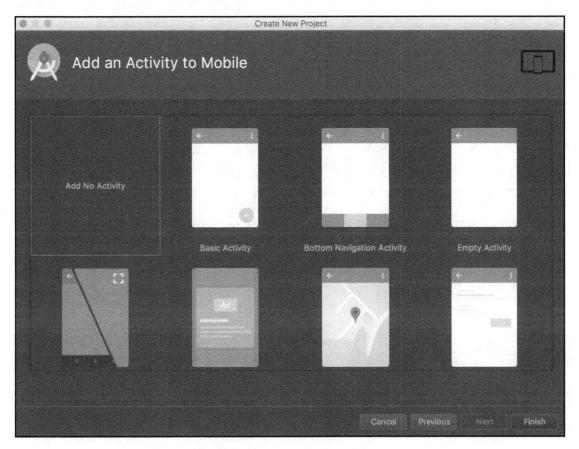

Once the project is created, let's add one **Empty Activity**. We can select different activity styles based on our needs:

Name the created activity **Launcher Activity** by selecting the checkbox. This adds an intent filter under the particular activity in the `AndroidManifest.xml` file:

```
<intent-filter>
    <action android:name="android.intent.action.MAIN" />
    <category android:name="android.intent.category.LAUNCHER" />
</intent-filter>
```

`<intent-filter>`: To advertise which implicit intents your app can receive, declare one or more intent filters for each of your app components with an `<intent-filter>` element in your manifest file. Each intent filter specifies the type of intents it accepts based on the intent's action, data, and category. The system delivers an implicit intent to your app component only if the intent can pass through one of your intent filters. Here, the intent is to keep this activity as the first activity when the app is opened by the user.

Next, we will name the launcher activity:

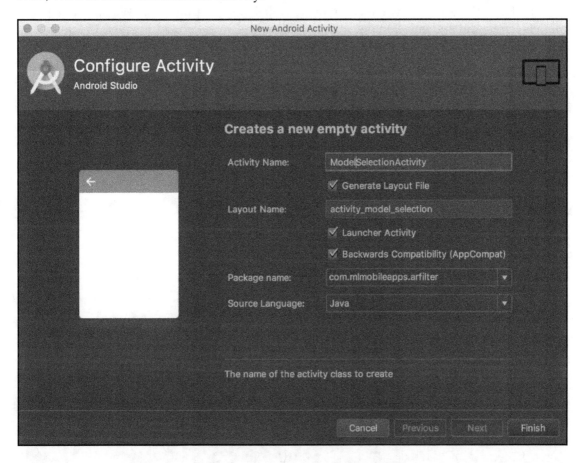

Once the activity is created, let's start designing the **user interface** (**UI**) layout for the activity. Here, the user selects which model to utilize in this application. We have two models for gender and emotion detection, whose details we discussed earlier. In this activity, we will add two buttons and their corresponding model classifiers, shown as follows:

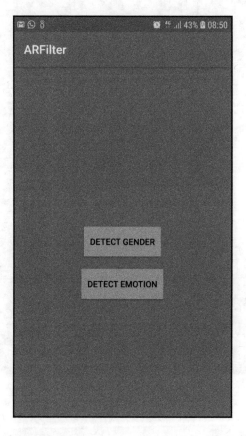

With the selection of the corresponding model, we will launch the next activity accordingly using a `clickListener` event with the `ModelSelectionActivity` class as follows. Based on the clicks on the buttons on gender identification or emotion identification, we will pass on the information to the `ARFilterActivity`. So that the corresponding model will be loaded into memory:

```
@Override
public void onClick(View view) {
    int id = view.getId();

    if(id==R.id.genderbtn){
```

```
        Intent intent = new Intent(this, ARFilterActivity.class);
        intent.putExtra(ARFilterActivity.MODEL_TYPE,"gender");
        startActivity(intent);
    }
    else if(id==R.id.emotionbtn){
        Intent intent = new Intent(this,ARFilterActivity.class);
        intent.putExtra(ARFilterActivity.MODEL_TYPE,"emotion");
        startActivity(intent);
    }
}
```

 Intent: An `Intent` is a messaging object you can use to request an action from another app component. Although intents facilitate communication between components in several ways, there are three fundamental use cases such as starting an `Activity`, starting a service and delivering a broadcast.

In `ARFilterActivity`, we will have the real-time `view` classification. The object that has been passed on will be received inside the filter activity, where the corresponding classifier will be invoked as follows. Based on the classifier selected from the previous activity, the corresponding model will be loaded into `ARFilterActivity` inside the `OnCreate()` method as shown as follows:

```
public static String classifierType(){
    String type = mn.getIntent().getExtras().getString("TYPE");
    if(type!=null) {
        if(type.equals("gender"))
            return "gender";
        else
            return "emotion";
    }
    else
        return null;
}
```

The UI will be designed accordingly in order to display the results in the bottom part of the layout via the `activity_arfilter` layout as follows. `CameraSourcePreview` initiates the Camera2 API for view inside that we will add `GraphicOverlay` class. It is a view which renders a series of custom graphics to be overlayed on top of an associated preview (that is the camera preview). The creator can add graphics objects, update the objects, and remove them, triggering the appropriate drawing and invalidation within the view.

It supports scaling and mirroring of the graphics relative the camera's preview properties. The idea is that detection items are expressed in terms of a preview size, but need to be scaled up to the full view size, and also mirrored in the case of the front-facing camera:

```
<com.mlmobileapps.arfilter.CameraSourcePreview
    android:id="@+id/preview"
    android:layout_width="wrap_content"
    android:layout_height="wrap_content">

    <com.mlmobileapps.arfilter.GraphicOverlay
        android:id="@+id/faceOverlay"
        android:layout_width="match_parent"
        android:layout_height="match_parent" />
</com.mlmobileapps.arfilter.CameraSourcePreview>
```

We use the `CameraPreview` class from the Google open source project and the `CAMERA` object needs user permission based on different Android API levels:

 Link to Google camera API: `https://github.com/googlesamples/android-Camera2Basic`.

Once we have the Camera API ready, we need to have the appropriate permission from the user side to utilize the camera as shown below. We need these following permissions:

- `Manifest.permission.CAMERA`
- `Manifest.permission.WRITE_EXTERNAL_STORAGE`

```
private void requestPermissionThenOpenCamera() {
    if(ContextCompat.checkSelfPermission(context,
Manifest.permission.CAMERA) == PackageManager.PERMISSION_GRANTED) {
        if (ContextCompat.checkSelfPermission(context,
Manifest.permission.WRITE_EXTERNAL_STORAGE) ==
PackageManager.PERMISSION_GRANTED) {
            Log.e(TAG, "requestPermissionThenOpenCamera:
                    "+Build.VERSION.SDK_INT);
            useCamera2 = (Build.VERSION.SDK_INT >=
Build.VERSION_CODES.LOLLIPOP);
            createCameraSourceFront();
        } else {
            ActivityCompat.requestPermissions(this, new String[]
{Manifest.permission.WRITE_EXTERNAL_STORAGE}, REQUEST_STORAGE_PERMISSION);
        }
    } else {
        ActivityCompat.requestPermissions(this, new
```

```
String[]{Manifest.permission.CAMERA}, REQUEST_CAMERA_PERMISSION);
    }
}
```

With this, we now have an application that has a screen where we can choose which model to load. On the next screen, we have the camera view ready. We now have to load the appropriate model, detect the face on the screen, and apply the filter accordingly.

Face detection on the real camera view is done through the Google Vision API. This can be added on your `build.gradle` as a dependency as follows. You should always use the latest version of the `api`:

```
api 'com.google.android.gms:play-services-vision:15.0.0'
```

The image classification object is initialized inside the `OnCreate()` method of the `ARFilterActivity` and inside the `ImageClassifier` class. The corresponding model is loaded based on user selection as follows:

```
private void initPaths(){
    String type = ARFilterActivity.classifierType();
    if(type!=null)
    {
        if(type.equals("gender")){
            MODEL_PATH = "gender.lite";
            LABEL_PATH = "genderlabels.txt";
        }
        else{
            MODEL_PATH = "emotion.lite";
            LABEL_PATH = "emotionlabels.txt";
        }
    }
}
```

Once the model is decided, we will read the file and load them into memory. The way to load the model is explained further. We will also read the model labels and read them into memory. Also we will allocate memory for the input image:

```
//tflite object is created with the model loaded into memory
tflite = new Interpreter(loadModelFile(activity));
//gets the list of defined labels for the model
labelList = loadLabelList(activity);
//input image buffer is created
imgData =
    ByteBuffer.allocateDirect(
        4 * DIM_BATCH_SIZE * DIM_IMG_SIZE_X * DIM_IMG_SIZE_Y *
DIM_PIXEL_SIZE);
imgData.order(ByteOrder.nativeOrder());
```

```
labelProbArray = new float[1][labelList.size()];
filterLabelProbArray = new float[FILTER_STAGES][labelList.size()];
```

The corresponding model is then loaded into memory from the `assets` folder as follows:

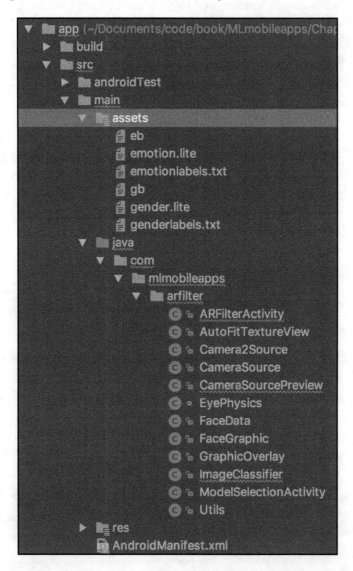

File descriptor of an entry in the `AssetManager`. This provides your own opened
`FileDescriptor` that can be used to read the data, as well as the offset and length of that
entry's data in the file. Assets folder is located besides our codebase main folder as shown
in the screenshot:

```
/** load the model into memory from Assets. */
private MappedByteBuffer loadModelFile(Activity activity) throws
IOException {
  AssetFileDescriptor fileDescriptor =
                        activity.getAssets().openFd(MODEL_PATH);
  FileInputStream inputStream = new
            FileInputStream(fileDescriptor.getFileDescriptor());
            FileChannel fileChannel = inputStream.getChannel();
            long startOffset = fileDescriptor.getStartOffset();
            long declaredLength = fileDescriptor.getDeclaredLength();
  return fileChannel.map(FileChannel.MapMode.READ_ONLY, startOffset,
declaredLength);
}
```

Once we have the model data loaded into memory, we need to have the corresponding
label file will be loaded into a list as follows. Labels files are located inside `Assets` folder
besides our model file:

```
/** Reads label list from Assets. */
private List<String> loadLabelList(Activity activity) throws IOException {
  List<String> labelList = new ArrayList<String>();
  BufferedReader reader =
      new BufferedReader(new
InputStreamReader(activity.getAssets().open(LABEL_PATH)));
  String line;
  while ((line = reader.readLine()) != null) {
    labelList.add(line);
  }
  reader.close();
  return labelList;
}
```

From the real-time camera view, frame-by-frame data is parsed by `ImageClassifier`. All
the ML algorithms and vision based libraries takes inputs into array of data. So we will
convert our input image data into ByteBuffer. The passed-on bitmap value will then be
converted into ByteBuffer as follows:

```
private void convertBitmapToByteBuffer(Bitmap bitmap) {
    if (imgData == null) {
      return;
    }
    imgData.rewind();
```

```
      bitmap.getPixels(intValues, 0, bitmap.getWidth(), 0, 0,
 bitmap.getWidth(), bitmap.getHeight());
      // Convert the image to floating point.
      int pixel = 0;
      long startTime = SystemClock.uptimeMillis();
      for (int i = 0; i < DIM_IMG_SIZE_X; ++i) {
        for (int j = 0; j < DIM_IMG_SIZE_Y; ++j) {
          final int val = intValues[pixel++];
          imgData.putFloat((((val >> 16) & 0xFF)-IMAGE_MEAN)/IMAGE_STD);
          imgData.putFloat((((val >> 8) & 0xFF)-IMAGE_MEAN)/IMAGE_STD);
          imgData.putFloat((((val) & 0xFF)-IMAGE_MEAN)/IMAGE_STD);
        }
      }
      long endTime = SystemClock.uptimeMillis();
 //    Log.d(TAG, "Timecost to put values into ByteBuffer: " +
 Long.toString(endTime - startTime));
    }
```

Then, the `classifyFrame()` method will be called. Once we have the input data as a `ByteBuffer`, we will call the TensorFlow Lite to classify the input by calling the `run()` method. This is where the magic happens:

```
convertBitmapToByteBuffer(bitmap);
// Here's where the magic happens!!!
long startTime = SystemClock.uptimeMillis();
tflite.run(imgData, labelProbArray);
long endTime = SystemClock.uptimeMillis();
Log.d(TAG, "Timecost to run model inference: " + Long.toString(endTime -
startTime));

// smooth the results
applyFilter();
```

 ByteBuffer is a baffling class. It is a bit like a RAM-based `RandomAccessFile`. It is also a bit like a ByteArrayList without the autogrow feature, to let you deal with partly filled `byte[]` in a consistent way. It has no asynchronous look-ahead. It is extremely low level. You must explicitly clear and fill the buffer and explicitly read/or write it. It is up to you to avoid overfilling the buffer.

Once we get the results from TensorFlow Lite model, we will start applying the filter. This is where we overlay corresponding filter on top of the camera view. Inside the `applyFilter` method, the corresponding label is assigned to the current frame and this is displayed on the screen as follows:

```
void applyFilter(){
  int num_labels = labelList.size();

  // Low pass filter `labelProbArray` into the first stage of the
      filter.
  for(int j=0; j<num_labels; ++j){
    filterLabelProbArray[0][j] += FILTER_FACTOR*(labelProbArray[0][j] -
filterLabelProbArray[0][j]);
  }
  // Low pass filter each stage into the next.
  for (int i=1; i<FILTER_STAGES; ++i){
    for(int j=0; j<num_labels; ++j){
      filterLabelProbArray[i][j] += FILTER_FACTOR*(
              filterLabelProbArray[i-1][j] -
              filterLabelProbArray[i][j]);
    }
  }

  // Copy the last stage filter output back to `labelProbArray`.
  for(int j=0; j<num_labels; ++j){
    labelProbArray[0][j] = filterLabelProbArray[FILTER_STAGES-1][j];
  }
}
```

We will print the top probability values on the view below the camera view. We have screenshots added as following. We will format the data and display it on the screen. Once the label is identified based on probability, the top labels are sent back as a result:

```
/** Prints top labels, to be shown in UI as the results. */
private String printTopKLabels() {
  for (int i = 0; i < labelList.size(); ++i) {
    sortedLabels.add(
        new AbstractMap.SimpleEntry<>(labelList.get(i),
labelProbArray[0][i]));
    if (sortedLabels.size() > RESULTS_TO_SHOW) {
      sortedLabels.poll();
    }
  }
  String textToShow = "";
  final int size = sortedLabels.size();
  for (int i = 0; i < size; ++i) {
    Map.Entry<String, Float> label = sortedLabels.poll();
    textToShow = String.format("\n%s: %3s",label.getKey(),
Math.round(label.getValue()*100) + "%"+textToShow);

    if(i==size-1)
      topLabel = label.getKey();
  }
```

```
        return textToShow;
    }
```

Now, let's go back to `ARFilterActivity`. With the Google Vision API, we detect the face inside each frame using `GraphicFaceTrackerFactory`. We will use `FaceDetector` from Google Vision API:

```
private void createCameraSourceFront() {
        previewFaceDetector = new FaceDetector.Builder(context)
                .setClassificationType(FaceDetector.NO_CLASSIFICATIONS)
                .setLandmarkType(FaceDetector.ALL_LANDMARKS)
                .setMode(FaceDetector.FAST_MODE)
                .setProminentFaceOnly(usingFrontCamera)
                .setTrackingEnabled(true)
                .setMinFaceSize(usingFrontCamera?0.35f : 0.15f)
                .build();

        if(previewFaceDetector.isOperational()) {
            previewFaceDetector.setProcessor(new
MultiProcessor.Builder<>(new GraphicFaceTrackerFactory()).build());
        } else {
            Toast.makeText(context, "FACE DETECTION NOT AVAILABLE",
                            Toast.LENGTH_SHORT).show();
        }
        Log.e(TAG, "createCameraSourceFront: "+useCamera2 );
        if(useCamera2) {
            mCamera2Source = new Camera2Source.Builder(context,
                                    previewFaceDetector)
                    .setFocusMode(Camera2Source.CAMERA_AF_AUTO)
                    .setFlashMode(Camera2Source.CAMERA_FLASH_AUTO)
                    .setFacing(Camera2Source.CAMERA_FACING_FRONT)
                    .build();
            startCameraSource();
        } else {
            mCameraSource = new CameraSource.Builder(context,
                                previewFaceDetector)
                    .setFacing(CameraSource.CAMERA_FACING_FRONT)
                    .setRequestedFps(30.0f)
                    .build();

            startCameraSource();
        }
    }
```

Parameters with `FaceDetector`:

- `ACCURATE_MODE`: Indicates a preference for accuracy in extended settings that may make an accuracy vs
- `ALL_CLASSIFICATIONS`: Performs *eyes open* and *smiling* classification
- `ALL_LANDMARKS`: Detects all landmarks
- `FAST_MODE`: Indicates a preference for speed in extended settings that may make an accuracy vs
- `NO_CLASSIFICATIONS`: Does not perform classification
- `NO_LANDMARKS`: Does not perform landmark detection

We detect all the facial points from there, and pass on the information in the `FaceData` class as follows:

```
// Get head angles.
mFaceData.setEulerY(face.getEulerY());
mFaceData.setEulerZ(face.getEulerZ());

// Get face dimensions.
mFaceData.setPosition(face.getPosition());
mFaceData.setWidth(face.getWidth());
mFaceData.setHeight(face.getHeight());

// Get the positions of facial landmarks.
mFaceData.setLeftEyePosition(getLandmarkPosition(face,
                                Landmark.LEFT_EYE));
mFaceData.setRightEyePosition(getLandmarkPosition(face,
                                Landmark.RIGHT_EYE));
mFaceData.setMouthBottomPosition(getLandmarkPosition(face,
                                Landmark.LEFT_CHEEK));
mFaceData.setMouthBottomPosition(getLandmarkPosition(face,
                                Landmark.RIGHT_CHEEK));
mFaceData.setNoseBasePosition(getLandmarkPosition(face,
                                Landmark.NOSE_BASE));
mFaceData.setMouthBottomPosition(getLandmarkPosition(face,
                                Landmark.LEFT_EAR));
mFaceData.setMouthBottomPosition(getLandmarkPosition(face,
                                Landmark.LEFT_EAR_TIP));
mFaceData.setMouthBottomPosition(getLandmarkPosition(face,
                                Landmark.RIGHT_EAR));
mFaceData.setMouthBottomPosition(getLandmarkPosition(face,
                                Landmark.RIGHT_EAR_TIP));
mFaceData.setMouthLeftPosition(getLandmarkPosition(face,
                                Landmark.LEFT_MOUTH));
mFaceData.setMouthBottomPosition(getLandmarkPosition(face,
```

```
                                    Landmark.BOTTOM_MOUTH));
mFaceData.setMouthRightPosition(getLandmarkPosition(face,
                                    Landmark.RIGHT_MOUTH));
```

Once all of the facial key points are identified, the corresponding decisions will be taken. We will take two decisions once a face is identified. We will first check whether the eyes are open and also we will check whether the person is smiling as follows:

```
// Decision: 1
//Identifies whether the eyes are open
final float EYE_CLOSED_THRESHOLD = 0.4f;
float leftOpenScore = face.getIsLeftEyeOpenProbability();
if (leftOpenScore == Face.UNCOMPUTED_PROBABILITY) {
    mFaceData.setLeftEyeOpen(mPreviousIsLeftEyeOpen);
} else {
    mFaceData.setLeftEyeOpen(leftOpenScore > EYE_CLOSED_THRESHOLD);
    mPreviousIsLeftEyeOpen = mFaceData.isLeftEyeOpen();
}
float rightOpenScore = face.getIsRightEyeOpenProbability();
if (rightOpenScore == Face.UNCOMPUTED_PROBABILITY) {
    mFaceData.setRightEyeOpen(mPreviousIsRightEyeOpen);
} else {
    mFaceData.setRightEyeOpen(rightOpenScore > EYE_CLOSED_THRESHOLD);
    mPreviousIsRightEyeOpen = mFaceData.isRightEyeOpen();
}

// Decision: 2
// identifies if person is smiling.
final float SMILING_THRESHOLD = 0.8f;
mFaceData.setSmiling(face.getIsSmilingProbability() > SMILING_THRESHOLD);
```

The detected facial data will then be passed on to a method that calculates the facial key point coordinates:

```
/** Given a face and a facial landmark position,
 *   return the coordinates of the landmark if known,
 *   or approximated coordinates (based on prior data) if not.
 */
private PointF getLandmarkPosition(Face face, int landmarkId) {
    for (Landmark landmark : face.getLandmarks()) {
        if (landmark.getType() == landmarkId) {
            return landmark.getPosition();
        }
    }

    PointF landmarkPosition =
            mPreviousLandmarkPositions.get(landmarkId);
    if (landmarkPosition == null) {
```

```
            return null;
        }

    float x = face.getPosition().x + (landmarkPosition.x *
                                      face.getWidth());
    float y = face.getPosition().y + (landmarkPosition.y *
                                      face.getHeight());
    return new PointF(x, y);
    }
```

Once all of this data is identified, we can then start applying the filter with the data that we have captured by overlaying the corresponding filter on top of the real-time camera view. The `GraphicOverlay` object will be passed on to the camera preview as follows:

```
private void startCameraSource() {
    if(useCamera2) {
        if(mCamera2Source != null) {
            cameraVersion.setText("Camera 2");
            try {mPreview.start(mCamera2Source, mGraphicOverlay);
            } catch (IOException e) {
                Log.e(TAG, "Unable to start camera source 2.", e);
                mCamera2Source.release();
                mCamera2Source = null;
            }
        }
    } else {
        if (mCameraSource != null) {
            cameraVersion.setText("Camera 1");
            try {mPreview.start(mCameraSource, mGraphicOverlay);
            } catch (IOException e) {
                Log.e(TAG, "Unable to start camera source.", e);
                mCameraSource.release();
                mCameraSource = null;
            }
        }
    }
}
```

Once the gender is identified, let's apply `GraphicOverlay` on the detected face. All of this filter-related magic is a result of the `FaceGraphic` class. Let's try applying a mustache image in between
the `noseBasePosition, mouthRightPosition, mouthLeftposition` coordinates:

```
drawMoustache(canvas,noseBasePosition,mouthLeftPosition,mouthRightPosition)
;
```

In the `draw` method, we define the container region for the overlay image as follows:

```
private void drawMoustache(Canvas canvas,
                           PointF noseBasePosition,
                           PointF mouthLeftPosition, PointF
mouthRightPosition) {
    int left = (int)mouthLeftPosition.x;
    int top = (int)noseBasePosition.y;
    int right = (int)mouthRightPosition.x;
    int bottom = (int) Math.min(mouthLeftPosition.y, mouthRightPosition.y);

    if (mIsFrontFacing) {
        mMustacheGraphic.setBounds(left, top, right, bottom);
    } else {
        mMustacheGraphic.setBounds(right, top, left, bottom);
    }
    mMustacheGraphic.draw(canvas);
}
```

In the real-time view, the applied graphic overlay will look as follows:

If the classifier finds a female in the image, it will draw a hat on top of their head instead of a mustache in order to differentiate from a male:

```
drawHat(canvas, position, width, height, noseBasePosition);
```

In the draw method, we define the container region for the overlay image as follows:

```
private void drawHat(Canvas canvas, PointF facePosition, float faceWidth,
float faceHeight, PointF noseBasePosition) {
    final float HAT_FACE_WIDTH_RATIO = (float)(4.0 / 4.0);
    final float HAT_FACE_HEIGHT_RATIO = (float)(3.0 / 6.0);
    final float HAT_CENTER_Y_OFFSET_FACTOR = (float)(1.0 / 8.0);

    float hatCenterY = facePosition.y + (faceHeight *
                        HAT_CENTER_Y_OFFSET_FACTOR);
    float hatWidth = faceWidth * HAT_FACE_WIDTH_RATIO;
    float hatHeight = faceHeight * HAT_FACE_HEIGHT_RATIO;

    int left = (int)(noseBasePosition.x - (hatWidth / 2));
    int right = (int)(noseBasePosition.x + (hatWidth / 2));
    int top = (int)(hatCenterY - (hatHeight / 2));
    int bottom = (int)(hatCenterY + (hatHeight / 2));
    mHatGraphic.setBounds(left, top, right, bottom);
    mHatGraphic.draw(canvas);
}
```

After drawing a hat, the applied graphic overlay will look like the following in the real-time view:

You can play with this some more by drawing a nose, mouth, rainbow puke, or anything you want on top of this!

References

- https://developers.google.com/vision/android/face-tracker-tutorial
- https://github.com/googlesamples/android-vision
- http://machinethink.net/blog/mobilenet-v2/
- https://github.com/googlesamples/android-Camera2Basic
- https://medium.com/tensorflow/using-tensorflow-lite-on-android-9bbc9cb7d69d

Questions

1. Can you build your own model on a different dataset?
2. Can you draw a different object instead of a hat or mustache?
3. Check whether you can detect any other object other than face detection and then apply a different filter on top of it.

Summary

With this app, you build an application feature that is similar to the one used on Snapchat or Instagram. If you are comfortable with OpenCV, you can detect a face without using Google APIs. With this, you can develop a lot of facelifting AR applications such as virtual makeup, virtual jewelry selection, virtual sunglass selection, and so on.

With this experience under your belt, let's move on to building an application that allows you to classify text for hand-drawn images.

In the next chapter, you will build an Android application that identifies freehand writing and classifies text based on numbers. We will use the MNIST database for this purpose.

6

Handwritten Digit Classifier Using Adversarial Learning

In this chapter, we will build an Android application that identifies free handwriting and classifies a number using adversarial learning. We will use the MNIST dataset for the digit classification. We will look into the basics of **Generative Adversarial Networks (GANs)**.

In this chapter, we will take a closer look at the following:

- GAN basics
- Understanding the **Modified National Institute of Standards and Technology (MNIST)** database
- Building a classifier
- Building an Android application

The code for this application can be found at `https://github.com/intrepidkarthi/MLmobileapps/tree/master/Chapter6`. and `https://github.com/PacktPublishing/Machine-Learning-Projects-for-Mobile-Applications`.

Generative Adversarial Networks

GANs are a class of **machine learning (ML)** algorithms used in unsupervised ML comprised of two deep neural networks contesting against each other (thus the word *adversarial*). GANs were introduced by Ian Goodfellow and other researchers at the University of Montreal, including Yoshua Bengio, in 2014.

Paper on GAN by Ian Goodfellow: `https://arxiv.org/abs/1406.2661`.

GANs have the potential to mimic any data. This means that GANs can be trained to create similar versions of any data such as images, audio, or text. As a quick example, Christie's sold a portrait generated by GANs for $432,000, based on open source code written by Robbie Barrat of Stanford.

A simple workflow of the GAN is shown in the following diagram:

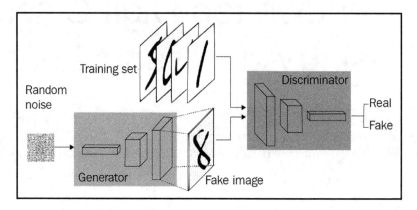

Generative versus discriminative algorithms

To understand GANs, we should know how discriminative and generative algorithms work. Discriminative algorithms try to predict a label and classify the input data or categorize them to where the data belongs. On the other hand, generative algorithms attempt to predict features given a certain label.

For example, a discriminative algorithm could predict whether an email message is spam or not spam. Here, *spam* is one of the labels, and the text captured from the message is considered the input data. If you consider the label as *y* and input as *x*, we can formulate this as follows:

$$p(y \mid x)$$

This means the probability of *y* given *x*, which translates to *the probability of an email is being spam given the words it contains*.

On the other hand, generative algorithms try to guess how likely these input features *x* are. Generative models care about *how you get x*, while discriminative models care about the relation between *y* and *x*.

As per our example in this chapter using the MNIST database, the generator will generate images and pass them on to the discriminator. The discriminator will authenticate the image if it is truly from the MNIST dataset. The generator generates images with the hope that it will pass through the discriminator with the hope that it will be authenticated even though it is fake as shown in the preceding diagram.

Steps in GAN

Based on our example, assume that we are passing numbers as inputs:

1. The generator takes random numbers as inputs and returns an image as the output.
2. The output image is passed into the discriminator and at the same time the discriminator receives input from the dataset as well.
3. The discriminator takes in both real and fake input images and returns probabilities between 0 and 1, with *1* representing a prediction of authenticity and *0* representing fake.

We have represented the same in our application by passing the user hand-drawn image as one of the fake images and try to get the probability value of it.

Understanding the MNIST database

The MNIST dataset consists of 60,000 handwritten digits. It also consists of a test dataset made up of 10,000 digits. While it is a subset of the NIST dataset, all the digits in this dataset are size-normalized and have been centered on a 28 x 28 pixels-sized image. Here every pixel contains a value of 0-255 with its grayscale value.

The MNIST dataset can be found at:
http://yann.lecun.com/exdb/mnist/.
The NIST dataset can be found at:
https://www.nist.gov/srd/nist-special-database-19.

Building the TensorFlow model

In this application, we will build an MNIST dataset-based TensorFlow model to be used in our Android application. Once we have the TensorFlow model, we will convert that into a TensorFlow Lite model. The step-by-step procedure on downloading the model and building the TensorFlow model is as follows.

Here is the architecture diagram on how our model works. The way to achieve the same is explained further:

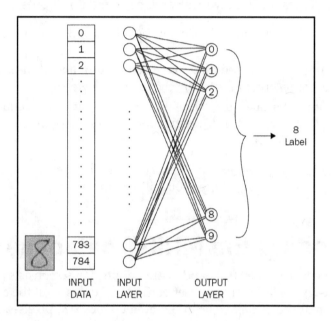

With TensorFlow, we can download the data with one line of Python code, as follows:

```
import tensorflow as tf
from tensorflow.examples.tutorials.mnist import input_data
# Reading data
mnist = input_data.read_data_sets("./data/", one_hot=True)
```

Now we have the MNIST dataset downloaded. After that, we will read the data as shown precedingly. Now we can run the script to download the dataset. We will run the script from the console as follows:

```
> python mnist.py
Successfully downloaded train-images-idx3-ubyte.gz 9912422 bytes.
Extracting MNIST_data/train-images-idx3-ubyte.gz
Successfully downloaded train-labels-idx1-ubyte.gz 28881 bytes.
```

```
Extracting MNIST_data/train-labels-idx1-ubyte.gz
Successfully downloaded t10k-images-idx3-ubyte.gz 1648877 bytes.
Extracting MNIST_data/t10k-images-idx3-ubyte.gz
Successfully downloaded t10k-labels-idx1-ubyte.gz 4542 bytes.
Extracting MNIST_data/t10k-labels-idx1-ubyte.gz
```

Once we have the dataset ready, we will add a few variables that we will use in our application as follows. We need to define these variables to control the parameters on building model on each layer which is required by the TensorFlow framework:

```
image_size = 28
labels_size = 10
learning_rate = 0.05
steps_number = 1000
batch_size = 100
```

This classification process is simple. The number of pixels that exist in a 28 x 28 image is 784. Thus, we have a corresponding number of input layers. Once we have the architecture set up, we will train the network and evaluate the results obtained to understand the effectiveness and accuracy of the model.

Now, let's define the variables that we have added precedingly. Depending on whether the model is in the training phase or the testing phase, different data will be passed through the classifier. The training process needs labels in order to be able to match them to current predictions. This is defined in a variable as follows:

```
# Define placeholders
training_data = tf.placeholder(tf.float32, [None,
                                image_size*image_size])
labels = tf.placeholder(tf.float32, [None, labels_size])
```

As the computation-graph evaluation occurs, placeholders will be filled. In the training process, we adjust the values of biases and weights toward increasing the accuracy of our results. To achieve it, we will define `weight` and `bias` parameters shown as follows:

```
# Variables to be tuned
W = tf.Variable(tf.truncated_normal([image_size*image_size,
                labels_size], stddev=0.1))
b = tf.Variable(tf.constant(0.1, shape=[labels_size]))
```

Once we have variables that can be tuned, we move on to build the output later in one step:

```
#Build the network (only output layer)
output = tf.matmul(training_data, W) + b
```

Training the neural network

By optimizing loss, we can get the training process to work. We need to reduce the difference between the actual label value and the network prediction; **cross-entropy** is the term used to define this loss.

In TensorFlow, cross-entropy is provided by the following method:

```
tf.nn.softmax_cross_entropy_with_logits
```

This method applies softmax on the model's prediction. Softmax is similar to logistic regression and produces a decimal between 0 and 1.0. For example, a logistic regression output of 0.9 from an email classifier suggests a 90% chance of an email being spam and a 10% chance of it not being spam. And the sum of all the probabilities is 1.0, as shown with an example in the following table.

Softmax is implemented through a neural network layer just before the output layer. The softmax layer must have the same number of nodes as the output layer:

Object	Probability
Apple	0.05
Car	0.80
Sunflower	0.01
Cup	0.14

Loss is defined using the `tf.reduce_mean` method and `GradientDescentOptimizer()` method is used in training steps to minimize the loss:

```
# Defining the loss
loss =
    tf.reduce_mean(tf.nn.softmax_cross_entropy_with_logits(labels=labels,
                logits=output))

# Training step with gradient descent
train_step =
        tf.train.GradientDescentOptimizer(learning_rate).minimize(loss)
```

The `GradientDescentOptimizer()` method will take several steps by adjusting the values of `W` and `b` (`weight` and `bias` parameters) in the output. The values will be adjusted till we reduce loss and are closer to more accurate prediction:

```
# Accuracy calculation
correct_prediction = tf.equal(tf.argmax(output, 1), tf.argmax(labels,
                              1))
accuracy = tf.reduce_mean(tf.cast(correct_prediction, tf.float32))
```

We start the training by initializing the session and the variables as follows:

```
# Run the training
sess = tf.InteractiveSession()
sess.run(tf.global_variables_initializer())
```

Based on the parameters on the number of steps defined previously, the algorithm will run with the training dataset. We run the optimizer on the number of steps, as follows:

```
for i in range(steps_number):
  # Get the next batch
  input_batch, labels_batch = mnist.train.next_batch(batch_size)
  feed_dict = {training_data: input_batch, labels: labels_batch}

  # Run the training step
  train_step.run(feed_dict=feed_dict)
```

With TensorFlow, we can measure the accuracy of our algorithm. We can print the accuracy value. We can keep it improving as long as the accuracy level increases and find the threshold value on where to stop as follows:

```
# Print the accuracy progress on the batch every 100 steps
  if i%100 == 0:
    train_accuracy = accuracy.eval(feed_dict=feed_dict)
    print("Step %d, batch accuracy %g %%"%(i, train_accuracy*100))
```

Once the training is done, we can evaluate the network's performance. We can use the training data to measure the performance:

```
# Evaluate on the test set
test_accuracy = accuracy.eval(feed_dict={training_data:
                   mnist.test.images, labels: mnist.test.labels})
print("Test accuracy: %g %%"%(test_accuracy*100))
```

When we run the Python script, the output on the console is as follows:

```
Step 0, training batch accuracy 13 %
Step 100, training batch accuracy 80 %
Step 200, training batch accuracy 87 %
Step 300, training batch accuracy 81 %
Step 400, training batch accuracy 86 %
Step 500, training batch accuracy 85 %
Step 600, training batch accuracy 89 %
```

```
Step 700, training batch accuracy 90 %
Step 800, training batch accuracy 94 %
Step 900, training batch accuracy 91 %
Test accuracy: 89.49 %
```

Now we have arrived at an accuracy rate of 89.2%; when we try to optimize our result more, the accuracy level reduces; this is where we have our threshold value to stop the training.

Let's build the TensorFlow model for the MNIST dataset. Inside the TensorFlow framework, the scripts provided save the MNIST dataset into a TensorFlow (.pb) model. The same script is attached to this application's repository.

 The code for this application can be found at https://github.com/ intrepidkarthi/MLmobileapps/tree/master/Chapter6 and https:// github.com/PacktPublishing/Machine-Learning-Projects-for-Mobile- Applications.

We begin by training the model using the following Python code line:

```
$:python mnist.py
```

We will run the script to generate our model. The following script helps us export the model by adding some additional parameters shown as follows:

```
python mnist.py --export_dir /./mnist_model
```

SavedModel can be found in the timestamped directory under /./mnist_model/ (for example, /./mnist_model/1536628294/).

The obtained TensorFlow model will be converted into a TensorFlow Lite model using toco, as follows:

```
toco \
  --input_format=TENSORFLOW_GRAPHDEF
  --output_format=TFLITE \
  --output_file=./mnist.tflite
  --inference_type=FLOAT \
  --input_type=FLOAT
  --input_arrays=x \
  --output_arrays=output
  --input_shapes=1,28,28,1 \
  --graph_def_file=./mnist.pb
```

Toco is a command-line tool to run **TensorFlow Lite Optimizing Converter** (**TOCO**) which converts a TensorFlow model into a TensorFlow Lite model. The preceding `toco` command produces `mnist.tflite` as output, which we will use in our application in the next section. We are not going deeper into options on the `toco` tool since it is discussed in detail at the other chapter.

Building the Android application

Let's create the Android application step by step with the model that we have built. We will start with creating a new project in Android Studio:

1. Create a new application in Android Studio:

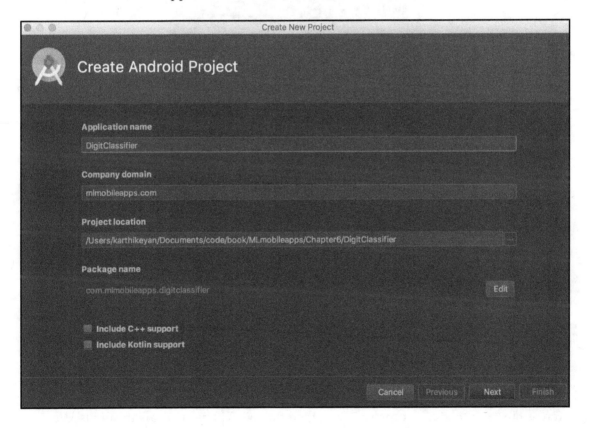

2. Drag the created TensorFlow Lite model to the `assets` folder along with the `labels.txt` file. We will read the model and label from the `assets` folder:

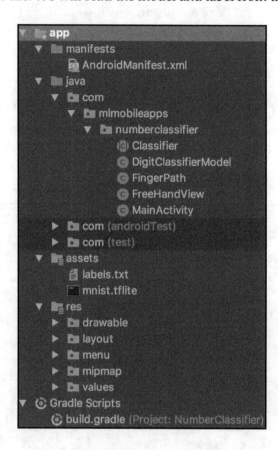

FreeHandView for writing

One of the advantages of this application is that we will create a simple view where users can draw any number of digits. In addition to this, the bar chart on the screen will show the classification of the detected number.

We will use step by step procedure to create the classifier.

Here is the `FreeHandView` constructor method that we will use to draw the digits. We initialize the `Paint` object with the necessary parameters, as follows:

```
public FreeHandView(Context context, AttributeSet attrs) {
    super(context, attrs);
    mPaint = new Paint();
    mPaint.setAntiAlias(true);
    mPaint.setDither(true);
    mPaint.setColor(DEFAULT_COLOR);
    mPaint.setStyle(Paint.Style.STROKE);
    mPaint.setStrokeJoin(Paint.Join.ROUND);
    mPaint.setStrokeCap(Paint.Cap.ROUND);
    mPaint.setXfermode(null);
    mPaint.setAlpha(0xff);

    mEmboss = new EmbossMaskFilter(new float[] {1, 1, 1}, 0.4f, 6,
                                    3.5f);
    mBlur = new BlurMaskFilter(5, BlurMaskFilter.Blur.NORMAL);
}
```

mPaint.setAntiAlias(true): Helper for setFlags(), setting or clearing the *ANTI_ALIAS_FLAG* bit. AntiAliasing smooths out the edges of what is being drawn, but is has no impact on the interior of the shape.
mPaint.setDither(true): Helper for setFlags(), setting or clearing the *DITHER_FLAG* bit. Dithering affects how colors that are higher precision than the device are down-sampled.
mPaint.setColor(DEFAULT_COLOR): Set the paint's color.
mPaint.setStyle(Paint.Style.STROKE): Set the paint's style, used for controlling how primitives' geometries are interpreted (except for drawBitmap, which always assumes Fill).
mPaint.setStrokeJoin(Paint.Join.ROUND): Set the paint's Join.
mPaint.setStrokeCap(Paint.Cap.ROUND): Set the paint's Cap.
mPaint.setXfermode(null): Set or clear the transfer mode object.
mPaint.setAlpha(0xff): Helper to setColor(), that only assigns the color's alpha value, leaving its r, g, b values unchanged.

Inside the init() method of the view life cycle, we will initialize ImageClassifier as well as pass on the BarChart object:

```
public void init(DisplayMetrics metrics, ImageClassifier classifier,
BarChart barChart) {
    int height = 1000;
    int width = 1000;
    mBitmap = Bitmap.createBitmap(width, height, Bitmap.Config.ARGB_8888);
    mCanvas = new Canvas(mBitmap);

    currentColor = DEFAULT_COLOR;
    strokeWidth = BRUSH_SIZE;
```

```
    mClassifier = classifier;
    this.predictionBar = predictionBar;
    this.barChart = barChart;
    addValuesToBarEntryLabels();
}
```

 We will use `Barchart` from the following library: `https://github.com/PhilJay/MPAndroidChart`.

We will initialize `Barchart` with *x* axis containing numbers from 0 to 9 and *y* axis containing the probability value from 0 to 1.0:

```
BarChart barChart = (BarChart) findViewById(R.id.barChart);
barChart.animateY(3000);
barChart.getXAxis().setEnabled(true);
barChart.getAxisRight().setEnabled(false);
barChart.getAxisLeft().setAxisMinimum(0.0f); // start at zero
barChart.getAxisLeft().setAxisMaximum(1.0f); // the axis maximum is 100
barChart.getDescription().setEnabled(false);
barChart.getLegend().setEnabled(false);

// the labels that should be drawn on the X-Axis
final String[] barLabels = new String[]{"0", "1", "2", "3", "4", "5", "6",
"7", "8", "9"};
//To format the value as integers
IAxisValueFormatter formatter = new IAxisValueFormatter() {

    @Override
    public String getFormattedValue(float value, AxisBase axis) {
        return barLabels[(int) value];
    }
};

barChart.getXAxis().setGranularity(0f); // minimum axis-step (interval) is
1
barChart.getXAxis().setValueFormatter(formatter);
barChart.getXAxis().setPosition(XAxis.XAxisPosition.BOTTOM);
barChart.getXAxis().setTextSize(5f);
```

Once we have initialized the view with Barchart, we will call the `OnDraw()` method of the view life cycle applies strokes in accordance with the path of the user's finger movements. `OnDraw()` method is called as part of the view life cycle method once after the view is initialized. Inside this, we will track the finger movement of the user and same is drawn on the canvas as explained follows:

```
@Override
protected void onDraw(Canvas canvas) {
    canvas.save();
    mCanvas.drawColor(backgroundColor);

    for (FingerPath fp : paths) {
        mPaint.setColor(fp.color);
        mPaint.setStrokeWidth(fp.strokeWidth);
        mPaint.setMaskFilter(null);

        if (fp.emboss)
            mPaint.setMaskFilter(mEmboss);
        else if (fp.blur)
            mPaint.setMaskFilter(mBlur);

        mCanvas.drawPath(fp.path, mPaint);
    }
    canvas.drawBitmap(mBitmap, 0, 0, mBitmapPaint);
    canvas.restore();
}
```

Inside the onTouchEvent() method, we track the user's finger position on move/up/down and initiate actions based on that. This is one of the method in the view's lifecycle to track the events. There are three events that will be triggered when you touch your mobile. We will trigger actions based on the finger movements. In the case of action_down and action_move, we will handle events to draw the on-hand movement on the view with the initial paint object attributes. When action_up event is triggered, we will save the view into a file as well as we will pass on the file image to the classifier to identify the digit and then we will represent the probability values using the barChart:

```
@Override
public boolean onTouchEvent(MotionEvent event) {
    float x = event.getX();
    float y = event.getY();
    BarData exampleData;

    switch(event.getAction()) {
        case MotionEvent.ACTION_DOWN :
            touchStart(x, y);
            invalidate();
            break;
        case MotionEvent.ACTION_MOVE :
            touchMove(x, y);
            invalidate();
            break;
        case MotionEvent.ACTION_UP :
            touchUp();
```

```
                       Bitmap scaledBitmap = Bitmap.createScaledBitmap(mBitmap,
                                   mClassifier.getImageSizeX(),
                                   mClassifier.getImageSizeY(), true);
                       Random rng = new Random();

                       try {
                           File mFile;
                           mFile =
                               this.getContext().getExternalFilesDir(String.valueOf
                               (rng.nextLong() + ".png"));
                           FileOutputStream pngFile = new FileOutputStream(mFile);
                       }
                       catch (Exception e){
                       }
                       //scaledBitmap.compress(Bitmap.CompressFormat.PNG, 90,
                                       pngFile);
                       Float prediction = mClassifier.classifyFrame(scaledBitmap);
                       exampleData = updateBarEntry();
                       barChart.animateY(1000, Easing.EasingOption.EaseOutQuad);
                       XAxis xAxis = barChart.getXAxis();
                       xAxis.setValueFormatter(new IAxisValueFormatter() {
                           @Override
                           public String getFormattedValue(float value, AxisBase
                   axis) {
                                   return xAxisLabel.get((int) value);
                           }
                       });
                       barChart.setData(exampleData);
                       exampleData.notifyDataChanged(); // let the data know a
                                                        // dataset changed
                       barChart.notifyDataSetChanged(); // let the chart know it's
                                                        // data changed
                       break;
                   }

               return true;
       }
```

Inside the ACTION_UP action, there is a method call for updateBarEntry(). This is where we call the classifier to get the probability of the result. This method also updates the BarChart based on the results from the classifier:

```
    public BarData updateBarEntry() {
        ArrayList<BarEntry> mBarEntry = new ArrayList<>();
        for (int j = 0; j < 10; ++j) {
            mBarEntry.add(new BarEntry(j, mClassifier.getProbability(j)));
        }
        BarDataSet mBarDataSet = new BarDataSet(mBarEntry, "Projects");
```

```
        mBarDataSet.setColors(ColorTemplate.COLORFUL_COLORS);
        BarData mBardData = new BarData(mBarDataSet);
        return mBardData;
    }
```

`FreeHandView` looks like this with an empty `BarChart`:

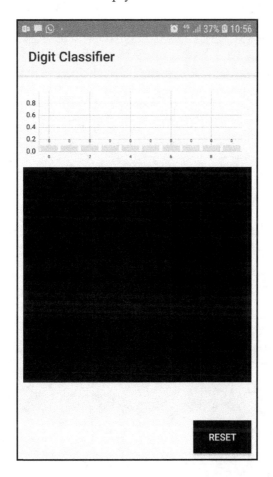

Digit classifier

Now let's write the classifier. Inside of this, we will first load the model file. This method reads the model from the `assets` folder and loads it into the memory:

```
/** Memory-map the model file in Assets. */
private MappedByteBuffer loadModelFile(Activity activity) throws
```

```
IOException {
    AssetFileDescriptor fileDescriptor =
                  activity.getAssets().openFd(getModelPath());
    FileInputStream inputStream = new
        FileInputStream(fileDescriptor.getFileDescriptor());
    FileChannel fileChannel = inputStream.getChannel();
    long startOffset = fileDescriptor.getStartOffset();
    long declaredLength = fileDescriptor.getDeclaredLength();
    return fileChannel.map(FileChannel.MapMode.READ_ONLY,
                        startOffset, declaredLength);
}
```

Now let's write the TensorFlow Lite classifier frame by frame. This is the place where we get the results from the digit classifier. Once we have received the saved file image of user input, the bitmap will be converted into byte buffer to run the inference on top of it. Once we have received the output, the time taken to get the results are noted using `SystemClock` time:

```
/** Classifies a frame from the preview stream. */
public float classifyFrame(Bitmap bitmap) {
    if (tflite == null) {
        Log.e(TAG, "classifier has not been initialized; Skipped.");
        return 0.5f;
    }

    convertBitmapToByteBuffer(bitmap);
    // Here's where the classification happens!!!
    long startTime = SystemClock.uptimeMillis();
    runInference();
    long endTime = SystemClock.uptimeMillis();
    Log.d(TAG, "Timecost to run model inference: " +
                    Long.toString(endTime - startTime));
    return getProbability(0);
}
```

The `runInference()` method calls the `run` method from `tflite`, as follows:

```
@Override
protected void runInference() {
    tflite.run(imgData, labelProbArray);
}
```

Next let's start the application from `MainActivity` where `barChart` is initialized.

Initialize `barChart` on the *x* and *y* axes along with the following values:

```
BARENTRY = new ArrayList<>();
initializeBARENTRY();
```

```
Bardataset = new BarDataSet(BARENTRY, "project");

BARDATA = new BarData(Bardataset);
barChart.setData(BARDATA);
```

Initialize `FreeHandView` to start classifying inside the `OnCreate()` method of `MainActivity`:

```
paintView.init(metrics, classifier, barChart);
```

When you reach the probability value of 1.00, the algorithm identifies the digit with 100% accuracy. An example of this is shown here:

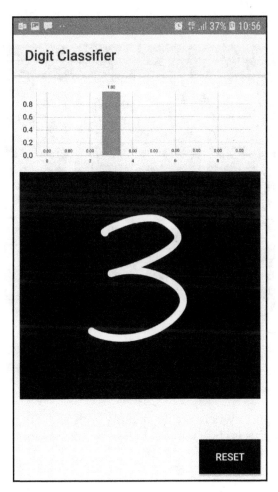

There are instances in which the classification has decreased probability with partial matches, as shown in the following screenshot:

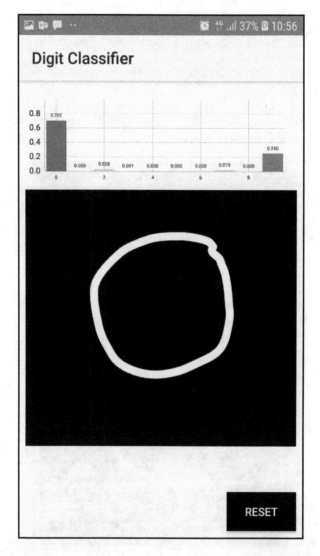

There are also other instances where the probability ends up with multiple partial matches. An example of this is shown in the following screenshot. Any such situation requires more rigorous training of the model:

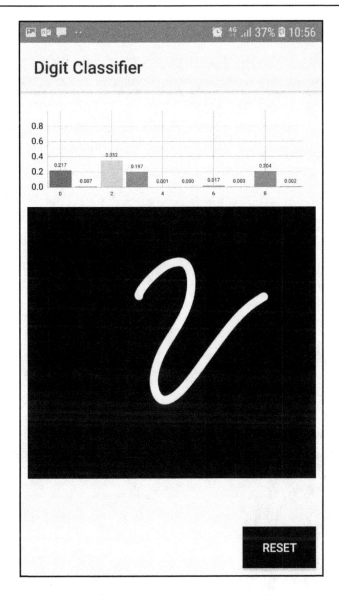

Clicking on the **RESET** button will clear up the view so that you can draw again. We will implement it using the following lines of code:

```
resetButton.setOnClickListener(new View.OnClickListener() {
    public void onClick(View v) {
        paintView.clear();
    }
});
```

Summary

Using this application, we can learn how to write a freehand writing classifier using TensorFlow Lite. With more data on handwritten alphabet datasets, we should be able to identify alphabets in any language using GAN.

In the next chapter, we will build a face-swapping application using OpenCV.

7
Face-Swapping with Your Friends Using OpenCV

Computer vision has come a long way. We can now recognize objects in order to generate a face-swapped video. This can be done by replacing one person's face with another person's face on a frame-by-frame basis. This process makes it difficult to detect whether a video is morphed or real.

In this chapter, we will look into building an application where an image of a face is placed on top of another image. We will also discuss the C++ toolkit containing **machine learning (ML)** algorithms called dlib and the **Open Source Computer Vision Library (OpenCV)**.

 OpenCV is a library that has C++, Python, and Java interfaces and supports Windows, Linux, macOS, iOS, and Android. OpenCV was designed for computational efficiency and with a focus on real-time applications. It is widely used across all vision-based applications. Dlib is a C++ toolkit containing ML algorithms and tools for creating real-world C++ based applications. It is used in both industry and academia in a wide range of domains, including robotics, embedded devices, mobile phones, and large high-performance computing environments. Dlib is open sourced, and it can be used in any application, free of charge.

The Android application created in this chapter uses both the frameworks along with Google Vision SDK for face detection in order to swap faces between two images. One simple example is shown in the following image:

 —  ←

The following topics will be covered in this chapter:

- Understanding how face-swapping works
- Building a native face-swapper library
- Building an Android application for face-swapping.

 The code block for this chapter can be found at `https://github.com/intrepidkarthi/MLmobileapps/tree/master/Chapter7` and `https://github.com/PacktPublishing/Machine-Learning-Projects-for-Mobile-Applications`.

Understanding face-swapping

For a long time, understanding human faces has been the grounds for research for computer vision engineers. The first application for this research came in the form of face recognition features. To identify a face in an input image or a video frame, our algorithm should first detect the location of the face. It will then cause a bounding box to frame a face in the image, as follows:

Once we have the bounding boxes, the obvious next step is to identify facial key points with more granular details inside the boxes, for example, the position of the eyes, the nose base, the eyebrows, and so on. Identifying facial landmark points will be helpful in building applications such as virtual makeup rooms, face morphing, **Augmented Reality (AR)** filters, and so on.

Facial key point identification made with the `dlib` library looks something like the following:

 Facial key point detection was initially invented by Vahid Kazemi and Josephine Sullivan, who identified 68 specific points that build up the facial landmarks, as shown in the preceding image. Here is the link to this paper: http://www.csc.kth.se/~vahidk/papers/KazemiCVPR14.pdf.

To apply face-swapping between two faces, there are a few things that we need to consider:

- Every picture will have different light settings, based on where it was taken. Alongside that, each person within the picture will have a different skin tone. This will make the images look different.
- Skin texture varies between people. For example, the skin texture of a child will usually be smooth, but this is not the case for an elderly person.

- Facial geometry differs for different people. If there is a huge difference between facial geometry, we may not receive the desired output. For example, if we try to swap the face of a 1-year old child with an 85-year old grandma, we may not get the desired output.
- Facial angle differs for different pictures. This depends on the camera angle as well.

Now let's jump into the step-by-step procedure involved in swapping two faces.

Steps in face-swapping

Face-swapping involves a step-by-step process of replacing one image with another. Once we understand the steps in face-swapping, we will build a native library to use in our application later in this chapter.

Facial key point detection

The important aspect that makes a face swap look real is aligning the face. The aim is to place one face on top of the other such that it covers the other face. To identify the facial key points, we need to identify the geometry of both faces. Since the geometry will be different between faces, we need to warp the source face to align it with the target face. Dlib helps with identifying 68 facial key points. We identify the outer boundary of the face as follows:

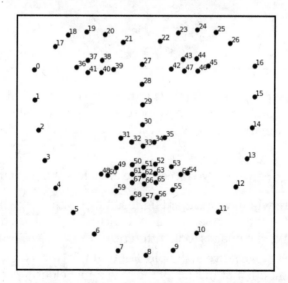

This image shows the 68 landmarks that are located on every face.

 The preceding image was created by Brandon Amos of CMU, who works on the `OpenFace` library.

Identifying the convex hull

Once we identify the key points, our next task is to find our convex hull. This is a boundary drawn around the facial key points. With the facial key points identified, we can find our hull by connecting the boundary points. A boundary that doesn't have any concavities is called a **convex hull**.

After applying the convex hull, the input image looks as follows:

Delaunay triangulation and Voronoi diagrams

The following image shows a regular image of a person on the left, the Delaunay triangulation of the image in the middle, and a Voronoi diagram of the same person on the right:

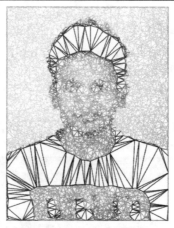

Given a set of points in a plane, a triangulation refers to the subdivision of the plane into triangles, with the points as vertices. For a set of points on the same line, there is no Delaunay triangulation. A set of points can have many possible triangulations, but Delaunay triangulation differs according to the condition that the circumcircles of all triangles have empty interiors.

Any discussions of Delaunay triangulation should draw upon the Voronoi diagram as these are both tightly coupled. The set of points that we calculate for triangulation is also used similarly with the Voronoi diagram:

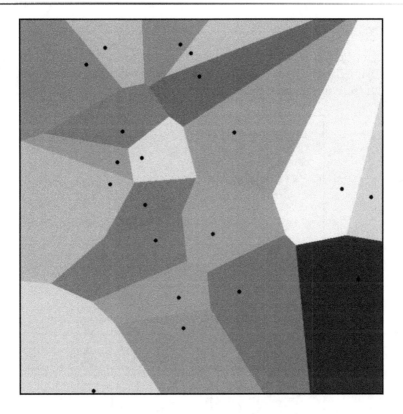

As you can see in the preceding image of a plane with a set of dots, a Voronoi diagram partitions the set of points into regions where the boundary lines are equidistant from neighboring dots. A Voronoi diagram is also referred to as Voronoi tessellation, Voronoi decomposition, Voronoi partition, or Dirichlet tessellation.

 The Wikipedia links to both these topics are https://en.wikipedia.org/wiki/Delaunay_triangulation and https://en.wikipedia.org/wiki/Voronoi_diagram.

Affine warp triangles

For each triangle found in the image, use the affine transform method to transform all pixels inside the triangle into a face-swapped image. Repeat this process until we get the warped version of the same image:

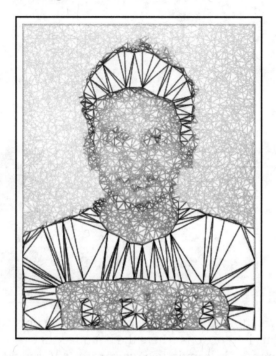

Similarly, do the same process on the second image to which the face is going to be swapped. This is achieved using an OpenCV method called `warpAffine`. We will look at this in detail when implementing the method.

After `warpAffine` is applied, the swapped images look as follows:

Seamless cloning

Up until the last step, the image swapped on top of another image may not look like it fits perfectly. To make the edges and the skin tone fit perfectly, we need to apply seamless cloning as the final step. There are three types of seamless cloning available, which are designed to make the best output of the final image:

- `NORMAL_CLONE`: This is the one we have used in our application. The power of the method is fully expressed when inserting objects with complex outlines into a new background.
- `MIXED_CLONE`: The classic method—color-based selection and alpha masking might be time-consuming, and it often leaves an undesirable halo.
- `FEATURE_EXCHANGE`: Feature exchange allows the user to easily replace certain features of one object with alternative features.

You have to pick what suits your application best:

With this, we get the perfect face-swapped image. Now it's time to start building the application.

Building the Android application

As a first step, we need to install **Native Development Kit** (**NDK**) with Android Studio. Since the core part of face-swapping involves native code in C++, NDK helps with building an Android application along with native code.

You can enable NDK inside the SDK manager under the **SDK Tools** tab, as shown in the following screenshot:

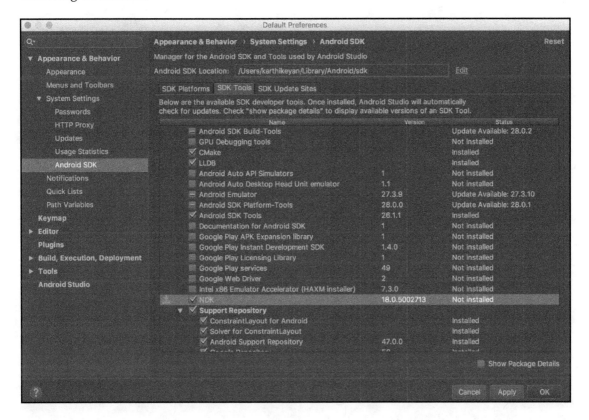

This library uses the OpenCV 3.0.0 version for Android SDK. This can be downloaded from `https://sourceforge.net/projects/opencvlibrary/files/opencv-android/3.0.0/`.

Building a native face-swapper library

Let us proceed to build the face-swapper library. Building a native library for Android involves three files:

- `Android.mk`
- `Application.mk`
- `faceswapper.cpp`

Creating a native library in Android is discussed here: `https://developer.android.com/ndk/guides/`.

Let's take a closer look at these before we begin building our model.

Android.mk

With this, change the `OpenCV.mk` path according to your local path. This application is built on MacBook Pro macOS High Sierra. The `Android.mk` file resides in the subdirectory of your project's `jni/` directory. It is really a tiny GNU `makefile` fragment that the build system parses once or more:

```
LOCAL_PATH := $(call my-dir)

include $(CLEAR_VARS)

OPENCV_INSTALL_MODULES:=on
OPENCV_CAMERA_MODULES:=off
OPENCV_LIB_TYPE:=STATIC
include /Users/karthikeyan/Downloads/OpenCV-
                        android/sdk/native/jni/OpenCV.mk

LOCAL_MODULE    := faceswapper
LOCAL_SRC_FILES := faceswapper.cpp
LOCAL_LDLIBS += -llog -ldl -landroid -latomic
LOCAL_CPPFLAGS := -O0 -g3 -std=c++11 -Wall -Wextra -fexceptions


include $(BUILD_SHARED_LIBRARY)
```

More information on the `Android.mk` file can be found here: `https://developer.android.com/ndk/guides/android_mk`.

Application.mk

`Application.mk` file contains the target ABIs, toolchain, release/debug mode, and STL. Default values of the few parameters are listed as follows if we don't specify them explicitly:

- **ABI**: All non-deprecated ABIs
- **Toolchain**: Clang
- **Mode**: Release
- **STL**: System

Here, we specify the toolchain, the Android API version, and the architecture that will be used. Similarly, if you are building for other architectures such as **Million Instructions Per Second** (**MIPS**), specify this in the `APP_ABI` variable as a comma-separated value:

```
NDK_TOOLCHAIN_VERSION := clang
APP_STL := gnustl_static
APP_CPPFLAGS := -frtti -fexceptions -std=c++11 -DNO_MAKEFILE
APP_ABI := armeabi-v7a
APP_PLATFORM := android-15

APP_CXX = -clang++
LOCAL_C_INCLUDES += ${ANDROID_NDK}/sources/cxx-stl/gnu-
libstdc++/4.8/include
```

The face-swapping logic is written in C++ using the OpenCV and dlib libraries.

 More details can be found here: `https://developer.android.com/ndk/guides/application_mk`.

Applying face-swapping logic

We will pass both the input images as arguments to the swapper method. Here `img1` is the image with face/s, and will be pasted onto the body/ies in `img2`. In general, `img2` contains the body/ies with faces, but the body will not be seen in the result. As a first step, we begin by feeding the method with the matrix values of both images along with all the point vectors (facial key points) calculated using dlib. We will get the warped image of `img2` shown as follows:

```
//faceswapper.cpp
Mat img1Warped = img2.clone();
```

```
//convert Mat to float data type
img1.convertTo(img1, CV_32F);
img1Warped.convertTo(img1Warped, CV_32F);

Mat img11 = img1, img22 = img2;
img11.convertTo(img11, CV_8UC3);
img22.convertTo(img22, CV_8UC3);
```

 CV_8UC3: Any primitive type from the list can be defined by an identifier in the form *CV_<bit-depth>{U | S | F}C(<number_of_channels>)* where U is an unsigned integer type, S is a signed integer type, and F is a float type. CV_8UC3 is an 8-bit unsigned integer matrix/image with three channels. Although it is most common that this means an RGB (or actually BGR) image, it does not mandate it. It simply means that there are three channels, and how you use them is up to you and your application.

After this, our next step is to identify the convex hull of the identified face polygon:

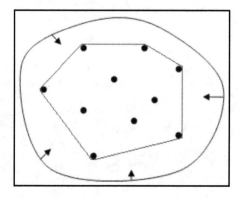

The convex hull of the polygon is the minimal convex set wrapping our polygon. For instance, when X is a bounded subset of the plane, the convex hull may be visualized as the shape enclosed by a rubber band stretched around X:

```
// Find convex hull
vector<Point2f> hull1;
vector<Point2f> hull2;
vector<int> hullIndex;

convexHull(points2, hullIndex, false, false);

for (size_t i = 0; i < hullIndex.size(); i++) {
    hull1.push_back(points1[hullIndex[i]]);
    hull2.push_back(points2[hullIndex[i]]);
}
```

Once the convex hull is identified, we will find the Delaunay triangulation using the following:

```
// Find delaunay triangulation for points on the convex hull
 vector< vector<int> > dt;
Rect rect(0, 0, img1Warped.cols, img1Warped.rows);
calculateDelaunayTriangles(rect, hull2, dt);
```

Once triangulation is complete, for each triangle found in the image, use the affine transform method to transform all pixels inside the triangle into a face-swapped image. Repeat this process until we get the warped version of the same image. We can warp image one and image two by using the following:

```
// Apply affine transformation to Delaunay triangles
for (size_t i = 0; i < dt.size(); i++) {
    vector<Point2f> t1, t2;
      // Get points for img1, img2 corresponding to the triangles
   for(size_t j = 0; j < 3; j++) {
      t1.push_back(hull1[dt[i][j]]);
      t2.push_back(hull2[dt[i][j]]);
   }
    warpTriangle(img1, img1Warped, t1, t2);
}

// Calculate mask
vector<Point> hull8U;
for (size_t i = 0; i < hull2.size(); i++) {
    Point pt(hull2[i].x, hull2[i].y);
    hull8U.push_back(pt);
}

Mat mask = Mat::zeros(img2.rows, img2.cols, img2.depth());
fillConvexPoly(mask, &hull8U[0], hull8U.size(), Scalar(255,255,255));
```

At the end of this step, we will get our unfinished output with different skin tones, which will look like unfinished output after swapping. To make the edges and the skin tone fit perfectly, we need to apply seamless cloning as the final step. To complete this cycle, we will apply seamless cloning as follows:

```
// Clone seamlessly.
Rect r = boundingRect(hull2);
img1Warped.convertTo(img1Warped, CV_8UC3);

Mat img1WarpedSub  = img1Warped(r);
Mat img2Sub        = img2(r);
Mat maskSub        = mask(r);
```

```
Point center(r.width/2, r.height/2);

Mat output;
int NORMAL_CLONE = 1;
seamlessClone(img1WarpedSub, img2Sub, maskSub, center, output,
NORMAL_CLONE);
```

Instead of `NORMAL_CLONE`, you can try passing values 2 and 3, which correspond to `MIXED_CLONE` and `FEATURE_EXCHANGE`.

This method will be called from the Android Java code base using the following:

```
Java_com_mlmobileapps_faceswapper_FaceSwap_portraitSwapNative(
                                JNIEnv *env,
                                jobject obj,
                                jlong addrImg1,
                                jlong addrImg2,
                                jintArray landmarksX1,
                                jintArray landmarksY1,
                                jintArray landmarksX2,
                                jintArray landmarksY2,
                                jlong addrResult )
{
    // Transform java points to readable OpenCV points
    vector<Point2f> points1 = readPoints(env, landmarksX1,
                                        landmarksY1);
    vector<Point2f> points2 = readPoints(env, landmarksX2,
                                        landmarksY2);

    // Get the OpenCV Mats
    Mat img1 = *(Mat*)addrImg1;
    Mat img2 = *(Mat*)addrImg2;
    Mat* retImg = (Mat*)addrResult;

    // Call faceswap function to swap faces
    Mat swapImg = faceswap_main(img1, img2, points1, points2);
    swapImg.convertTo(swapImg, CV_8UC3);
    swapImg.copyTo(*retImg);
}
}
```

Save the C++ file as `faceswapper.cpp`.

Now it is time to build the library. From the Terminal, run the following command:

```
$ndk-build V=1
```

You will find the `libfaceswapper.so` library generated inside the corresponding architecture folder. Copy the file inside the `jnilibs` folder of the Android project. We will not go into every single layout generated with the project. Instead, you can download the complete code base from our common code repository on GitHub.

 GitHub link: `https://github.com/intrepidkarthi/MLmobileapps/tree/master/Chapter7` and `https://github.com/PacktPublishing/Machine-Learning-Projects-for-Mobile-Applications`.

Building the application

It is easier to create the UI using design editor inside Android Studio. If you are comfortable with XML-based text editor, you can use that as well. We will create a simple `ViewPager` (`activity_swap.xml`) that will hold two input images inside a `CoordinatorLayout` as shown in the following code block:

```
<android.support.v4.view.ViewPager
    android:id="@+id/container"
    android:layout_width="0dp"
    android:layout_height="0dp"
    android:layout_gravity="center_vertical"
    app:layout_behavior="@string/appbar_scrolling_view_behavior"
    app:layout_constraintBottom_toTopOf="@+id/container1"
    app:layout_constraintHorizontal_bias="0.0"
    app:layout_constraintLeft_toLeftOf="parent"
    app:layout_constraintRight_toRightOf="parent"
    app:layout_constraintTop_toBottomOf="@+id/container2"/>
```

And we need `TabLayout` to hold the `ViewPager` views in it. We will add it inside `AppBarLayout` preceding the `ViewPager` shown as follows:

```
<android.support.design.widget.AppBarLayout
    android:id="@+id/appbar"
    android:layout_width="0dp"
    android:layout_height="wrap_content"
    android:paddingTop="@dimen/appbar_padding_top"
    android:theme="@style/AppTheme.AppBarOverlay"
    app:layout_constraintHorizontal_bias="0.0"
    app:layout_constraintLeft_toLeftOf="parent"
    app:layout_constraintRight_toRightOf="parent"
```

```
app:layout_constraintTop_toBottomOf="@+id/main_toolbar">

    <android.support.design.widget.TabLayout
        android:id="@+id/tabs"
        android:layout_width="match_parent"
        android:layout_height="wrap_content"
        android:fillViewport="false"
        app:tabGravity="fill"
        app:tabMaxWidth="0dp"
        app:tabMode="fixed" />

</android.support.design.widget.AppBarLayout>
```

Once we have the layouts ready, we will initialize the same inside `FaceSwapperActivity`. Create the adapter that will return a fragment for each of the three primary sections of the activity shown as follows:

```
private void setupTabs() {
    mSectionsPagerAdapter = new
                SectionsPagerAdapter(getSupportFragmentManager());

    // Set up the ViewPager with the sections adapter.
    mViewPager = (ViewPager) findViewById(R.id.container);
    mViewPager.setAdapter(mSectionsPagerAdapter);

    tabLayout = (TabLayout) findViewById(R.id.tabs);
    tabLayout.setupWithViewPager(mViewPager);
    // Sets tab icons
tabLayout.getTabAt(0).setIcon(ResourcesCompat.getDrawable(getResources(
                    ), R.drawable.ic_face, null));
    tabLayout.getTabAt(1).setIcon(ResourcesCompat.getDrawable(getResources(
                    ), R.drawable.ic_face, null));

    tabLayout.addOnTabSelectedListener(this);
}
```

Once we have the tabs setup, we will add buttons to snap pictures and, pick gallery images as well as to call the swapping method. With that, we will add controls to snap pictures from the camera and pick images from the user photo gallery.

Before writing any actions on the buttons, we need to check whether we have permission to snap pictures and have read/write permissions in the storage area to pick images from the gallery, shown as follows:

```
/**
 * Controls if an app has permission to use the camera and internal
storage.
```

```
@return true if permissions are ok otherwise false.
 */
private boolean checkPermissions() {
    granted = true;
    // List the permissions
    String requests[] = {
            Manifest.permission.CAMERA,
            Manifest.permission.READ_EXTERNAL_STORAGE,
            Manifest.permission.WRITE_EXTERNAL_STORAGE,
    };

    for (String request : requests) {
        if (ContextCompat.checkSelfPermission(this, request) !=
PackageManager.PERMISSION_GRANTED) {
            granted = false;
        }
    }
    if (granted) {
        return true;
    }
    ActivityCompat.requestPermissions(this, requests,
                        MY_PERMISSIONS_REQUEST_READ_CONTACTS);
    return granted;
}
```

Once we have the permission setup right, we will add actions to the buttons for camera and the gallery image picker. The following code starts the camera and captures the view as an image:

```
@SuppressWarnings("UnusedParameters")
public void cameraMode(View view) {
    if (checkPermissions()) {
        Intent intent = new Intent(MediaStore.ACTION_IMAGE_CAPTURE);
        if (Build.VERSION.SDK_INT >= CAMERA_API_LEVEL_LIMIT) {
            //for api > = 24
            File file = createImageFile();
            if (file != null) {
                Uri photoURI =
FileProvider.getUriForFile(getApplicationContext(),
BuildConfig.APPLICATION_ID + ".provider", file);

                intent.putExtra(MediaStore.EXTRA_OUTPUT, photoURI);
            }

        } else {
            //api < 24
            intent = new Intent(MediaStore.ACTION_IMAGE_CAPTURE);
            intent.putExtra(MediaStore.EXTRA_OUTPUT,
```

```
                            getPhotoFileUri());

        // Avoid crash
        if (intent.resolveActivity(getPackageManager()) != null) {
            // Start the image capture intent to take photo
            startActivityForResult(intent,
                    CAPTURE_IMAGE_ACTIVITY_REQUEST_CODE);
        }
    }
    // Avoid crash
    if (intent.resolveActivity(getPackageManager()) != null) {
        // Start the image capture intent to take photo
        startActivityForResult(intent,
                CAPTURE_IMAGE_ACTIVITY_REQUEST_CODE);
    }
} else {
    if (infoToast != null) {
        infoToast.cancel();
    }
    infoToast = showInfoToast(getString(R.string.err_permission));
}
}
```

There is also an option to pick an image from the photo gallery. Once we get the resultant picked or snapped image, we will call `startActivityForResult` method as shown as follows:

```
@SuppressWarnings("UnusedParameters")
public void galleryMode(View view) {
    if (checkPermissions()) {
        // Opens photo album
        Intent i = new Intent(Intent.ACTION_PICK,
MediaStore.Images.Media.EXTERNAL_CONTENT_URI);
        startActivityForResult(i, RESULT_LOAD_IMAGE);
    } else {
        if (infoToast != null) {
            infoToast.cancel();
        }
        infoToast = showInfoToast(getString(R.string.err_permission));
    }
}
```

Once we have all the basic UI layouts setup, the application will look as follows:

The native library will be loaded inside the application using a `FaceSwap` class:

```
 * @param addrImg1,     memory address to image 1.
 * @param addrImg2,     memory address to image 2.
 * @param landmarksX1, facial landmark x-coordinates to image 1.
 * @param landmarksY1, facial landmark y-coordinates to image 1.
 * @param landmarksX2, facial landmark x-coordinates to image 2.
 * @param landmarksY2, facial landmark y-coordinates to image 2.
 * @param addrResult, memory address to result image.
 */
@SuppressWarnings("JniMissingFunction")
public native void portraitSwapNative(long addrImg1,
                                      long addrImg2,
                                      int[] landmarksX1,
                                      int[] landmarksY1,
                                      int[] landmarksX2,
                                      int[] landmarksY2,
                                      long addrResult);


/* Load Native Library */
static {
    //noinspection StatementWithEmptyBody
    if (!OpenCVLoader.initDebug()) ;
    else System.loadLibrary("faceswapper");
}
```

After that, we write the method to be called when face-swapping. We need to pass on all the facial key points as an input to the method. We can get the facial data from Google Vision SDK using the `FaceDetector` class:

```
FaceDetector detector = new FaceDetector.Builder(context)
        .setTrackingEnabled(false)
        .setLandmarkType(FaceDetector.ALL_LANDMARKS)
        .build();
```

From the library, we will find all the landmark points. A list of landmarks follows. This is used to identify a face from the given input image:

```
case Landmark.RIGHT_CHEEK:
    x1 = (float) (x1 + 0.8 * FACE_CONST * faceW * Math.cos(Math.PI +
theta));
    y1 = (float) (y1 + FACE_CONST * faceW * Math.sin(Math.PI + theta));

    xRightEye += x1;
    yRightEye += y1;
    break;

case Landmark.LEFT_CHEEK:
```

```
        x1 = (float) (x1 + 0.8 * FACE_CONST * faceW * Math.cos(theta));
        y1 = (float) (y1 + FACE_CONST * faceW * Math.sin(theta));

        xLeftEye += x1;
        yLeftEye += y1;
        break;

    case Landmark.RIGHT_MOUTH:
        x1 = (float) (x1 + 0.75 * FACE_CONST * faceW * Math.cos((-Math.PI /
                    8) + Math.PI + theta));
        y1 = (float) (y1 + 0.75 * FACE_CONST * faceW * Math.sin((-Math.PI /
                    8) + Math.PI + theta));

        xMouthRight += x1;
        yMouthRight += y1;
        break;

    case Landmark.LEFT_MOUTH:
        x1 = (float) (x1 + 0.75 * FACE_CONST * faceW * Math.cos(Math.PI / 8
                    + theta));
        y1 = (float) (y1 + 0.75 * FACE_CONST * faceW * Math.sin(Math.PI / 8
                    + theta));

        xMouthLeft += x1;
        yMouthLeft += y1;
        break;

    case Landmark.BOTTOM_MOUTH:
        x1 = (float) (x1 + FACE_CONST_MOUTH * faceW * Math.cos(theta90));
        y1 = (float) (y1 + FACE_CONST_MOUTH * faceW * Math.sin(theta90));

        xMouthLeft += x1;
        xMouthRight += x1;
        yMouthLeft += y1;
        yMouthRight += y1;
        break;
```

Landmarks are on the eyes are handled as shown as follows:

```
    case Landmark.RIGHT_EYE:
        x1 = (float) (x1 + 1.05 * FACE_CONST_EYE * faceW * Math.cos(Math.PI
                    + Math.PI / 5 + theta));
        y1 = (float) (y1 + FACE_CONST_EYE * faceW * Math.sin(Math.PI +
                    Math.PI / 5 + theta));

        xRightEye += x1;
        yRightEye += y1;
```

```
        xForeHeadMid += x1;
        yForeHeadMid += y1;
        xForeHeadRight += x1;
        yForeHeadRight += y1;
        break;

    case Landmark.LEFT_EYE:
        x1 = (float) (x1 + 1.05 * FACE_CONST_EYE * faceW * Math.cos(-
                    Math.PI / 5 + theta));
        y1 = (float) (y1 + FACE_CONST_EYE * faceW * Math.sin(-Math.PI / 5 +
                    theta));

        xLeftEye += x1;
        yLeftEye += y1;
        xForeHeadMid += x1;
        yForeHeadMid += y1;
        xForeHeadLeft += x1;
        yForeHeadLeft += y1;
        break;
```

Once we have all the facial key coordinates, we call the `swap` method, which internally calls the native library `swap` method:

```
/**
 * Swaps the faces of two photos where the faces have landmarks pts1 and
pts2.
 *
 * @param bmp1 photo 1.
 * @param bmp2 photo 2.
 * @param pts1 landmarks for a face in bmp1.
 * @param pts2 landmarks for a face in bmp2.
 * @return a bitmap where a face in bmp1 has been pasted onto a face in
    bmp2.
 */
private Bitmap swap(Bitmap bmp1, Bitmap bmp2, ArrayList<PointF> pts1,
                ArrayList<PointF> pts2) {
    // For storing x and y coordinates of landmarks.
    // Needs to be stored like this when sending them to native code.
    int[] X1 = new int[pts1.size()];
    int[] Y1 = new int[pts1.size()];
    int[] X2 = new int[pts2.size()];
    int[] Y2 = new int[pts2.size()];

    for (int i = 0; i < pts1.size(); ++i) {
        int x1 = pts1.get(i).X();
        int y1 = pts1.get(i).Y();
        X1[i] = x1;
        Y1[i] = y1;
```

```
        int x2 = pts2.get(i).X();
        int y2 = pts2.get(i).Y();
        X2[i] = x2;
        Y2[i] = y2;
    }

    // Get OpenCV data structures
    Mat img1 = new Mat();
    bitmapToMat(bmp1, img1);
    Mat img2 = new Mat();
    bitmapToMat(bmp2, img2);

    // Convert to three channel image format
    Imgproc.cvtColor(img1, img1, Imgproc.COLOR_BGRA2BGR);
    Imgproc.cvtColor(img2, img2, Imgproc.COLOR_BGRA2BGR);

    Mat swapped = new Mat();
    // Call native function to get swapped image
    portraitSwapNative(img1.getNativeObjAddr(), img2.getNativeObjAddr(),
X1, Y1, X2, Y2, swapped.getNativeObjAddr());
    // Convert back to standard image format
    Bitmap bmp = Bitmap.createBitmap(bmp1.getWidth(), bmp1.getHeight(),
Bitmap.Config.ARGB_8888);
    matToBitmap(swapped, bmp);

    return bmp;
}
```

Similarly, we can swap multiple images from a single image as follows:

```
/**
 * Makes a group face swap, swaps faces in an image.
 * Callers make sure bitmap is not null.
 * @param bitmap image with faces, #faces >= 2
 * @return status.
 */
fsStatus multiSwap(Bitmap bitmap) {
    // Get facial landmarks for people in bitmap
    ArrayList<ArrayList<PointF>> landmarks = getFacialLandmarks(bitmap);

    // Check if people were found (at least 2)
    if (landmarks.size() < 2) return fsStatus.FACE_SWAP_TOO_FEW_FACES;

    if (landmarks.size() == 2) {
        if (landmarks.get(0).size() != LANDMARK_SIZE)
            return fsStatus.FACE_SWAP_INSUFFICIENT_LANDMARKS_IMAGE1;

        if (landmarks.get(1).size() != LANDMARK_SIZE)
```

```
                    return fsStatus.FACE_SWAP_INSUFFICIENT_LANDMARKS_IMAGE1;
    }

    Bitmap bitmap1 = bitmap.copy(bitmap.getConfig(), true);
    Bitmap bitmap2 = bitmap.copy(bitmap.getConfig(), true);

    int faceSwapCount = 0;

    // Start swapping faces
    int i = 0;
    while (i < landmarks.size() - 1) {

        if (landmarks.get(i).size() != LANDMARK_SIZE) {
            i++;
        } else {

            bitmap2 = swap(bitmap1, bitmap2, landmarks.get(i),
landmarks.get(i + 1));
            bitmap2 = swap(bitmap1, bitmap2, landmarks.get(i + 1),
landmarks.get(i));

            faceSwapCount++;
            i += 2;
        }
    }

    // An extra swap if the number of faces is odd.
    if (landmarks.size() % 2 == 1) {
        int ind = landmarks.size();
        if (landmarks.get(ind - 2).size() == LANDMARK_SIZE &&
landmarks.get(ind - 2).size() == LANDMARK_SIZE) {
            bitmap2 = swap(bitmap2, bitmap2, landmarks.get(ind - 2),
landmarks.get(ind - 1));
            bitmap2 = swap(bitmap1, bitmap2, landmarks.get(ind - 1),
landmarks.get(ind - 2));
            faceSwapCount++;
        }
    }
    if (faceSwapCount == 0) return fsStatus.FACE_SWAP_TOO_FEW_FACES;
    res = bitmap2;
    return fsStatus.FACE_SWAP_OK;
}
```

We will now start loading the images as inputs. We can either pick an image from the camera or from the gallery:

Both images are now loaded. Once we have loaded both images, we can swap them. The output is as follows:

For a better output, use images of the same resolution and size. If the bounding box contains data of the same size, you will get a better output. The skin tone and image geometry also play an important role here.

If you face any issues when compiling the code, try disabling NDK from the SDK manager and trying again.

Summary

In this chapter, we have learned how to build a complete face-swapping application. This is one of the basic components of computer vision research. A lot of useful applications can be built on top of this.

In the next chapter, we will build our own food classifier using TensorFlow as well as building that into an iOS application using Core ML.

References

There have been a lot of trending discussions about face-swapping. For more information, see the following:

- Face-swapping with deep learning: https://github.com/deepfakes/faceswap
- Image scrapper from the Google and Bing API: https://github.com/rushilsrivastava/image_search
- Python implementation with dlib and OpenCV framework of the same application: https://github.com/wuhuikai/FaceSwap
- Face-swapping with GAN: https://github.com/shaoanlu/faceswap-GAN

Questions

1. Did you understand how face swapping is done?
2. Can you build a NDK library for Android yourself?
3. Can you build a simple Android app with `ViewPager`?
4. Can you build a complete face swapping/morphing application?

8
Classifying Food Using Transfer Learning

In this chapter, we are going to classify food items using **transfer learning**. For this, we have built our own TensorFlow-based **machine learning** (**ML**) model of some Indian food items that we will focus on. Millions of parameters are there with the modern recognition models. We need a lot of time and data to train a new model from scratch, as well as hundreds of **Graphical Processing Units** (**GPUs**) or **Tensor Processing Units** (**TPUs**) that run for hours.

Transfer learning makes this task easier by using an existing model that is already trained and reusing it on a new model. In our example, we will use the feature extraction capabilities from the MobileNet model and train our own classifier on top of it. Even if we don't get 100% accuracy, this works best in a lot of cases and especially on a mobile phone, where we don't get heavy resources. We can easily train this model on a typical laptop for a few hours even without a GPU. This model is built on a MacBook Pro with a 2.6 GHZ Intel i5 processor and 8 GB RAM.

In this chapter, we will take a closer look at the following:

- Basics on Transfer learning
- Training our own TensorFlow model
- Building an iOS app that consumes the model

 The code for the complete chapter can be pulled directly from `https://github.com/intrepidkarthi/MLmobileapps/tree/master/Chapter8` and `https://github.com/PacktPublishing/Machine-Learning-Projects-for-Mobile-Applications`.

Transfer learning

Transfer learning is one of the popular approach in deep learning where a model developed for one task is reused for another model on a different task. Here pre-trained models are used as a first step on computer vision based tasks or **natural language processing** (NLP) based tasks provided we have very limited computational resources and time.

In a typical computer vision based problem, neural networks try to detect edges in their initial level layers, shapes in the middle level layers and more specific features in the final level layers. With transfer learning, we will use the initial and middle level layers and only re-train the final level layers.

For example, if we have a model trained to recognize an apple from the input image, it will be reused to detect water bottles. In the initial layers, the model has been trained to recognize objects so we will retrain only the final level layers. In that way, our model will learn what will differentiate water bottle from other objects:

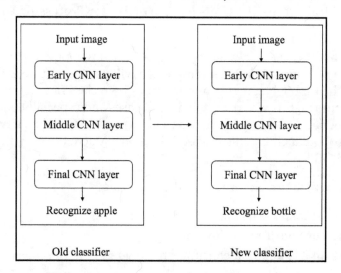

Typically we need a lot of data to train our model but most of the time we will not have enough relevant data. That is where transfer learning comes into picture where you can train your model with very less amount of data.

If your old classifier was developed and trained using TensorFlow, you can reuse the same to retrain a few of the layers for your new classifier. This will work perfectly only if the features learned from the old task is more generic in nature. For example, you can't reuse a model developed for a text classifier on an image classification based task. Also the input data size should match for both the models. If the sizes doesn't match, we need to add an additional pre-processing step to resize the input data accordingly.

Approaches in transfer learning

Lets look into different approaches to transfer learning. There could be different names given to the approaches but the concept remains the same:

1. **Use a pre-trained model**: There are a lot of pre-trained models out there to satisfy your basic deep learning research. In this book, we have used a lot of pre-trained models from where we derive our results.

2. **Train a model for reuse**: Assume you wants to solve problem A but you don't have enough data to achieve the results. To solve the issue, we have another problem B where we have enough amount of data. In that case, we can develop a model for problem B and use the model as a starting point for problem A. If we need to reuse all the layers or only a few layers is dependent on the type of problem that we are solving.

3. **Feature extraction**: With deep learning, we can extract the features of the data set. Most of the time, the features are hand-crafted by the developers. Neural Networks have the ability to learn which features, you have to pass and which one you don't. For example, we will only use the initial layers to detect the right representation of features but we will not use the output because it might be more specific to one particular task. We will simply feed the data into our network and use one of the immediate middle level layer as the output layer.

With this we will start building our model using TensorFlow.

Training our own TensorFlow model

Building our own custom model requires following a step-by-step procedure. To begin, we are going to use the TensorFlow Hub to feed images using pre-trained models.

 TensorFlow Hub is a library for the publication, discovery, and consumption of reusable parts of machine learning models. A *module* is a self-contained piece of a TensorFlow graph, along with its weights and assets, that can be reused across different tasks in a process known as **transfer learning**.

Installing TensorFlow

While writing this book, TensorFlow 1.7.0 was available. The TensorFlow Hub has a dependency on the TensorFlow library and can be installed with `pip` as follows:

```
$ pip install "tensorflow>=1.7.0"
$ pip install tensorflow-hub
```

When the TensorFlow library is installed, we need to start collecting our image dataset before the training process starts. We need to look into a lot of things before beginning our training.

Training the images

In this step, we will collect the images and keep them organized under the respective category of folders.

A few common steps for choosing your own dataset of images are as follows:

1. First of all, we need at least 100 photos of each image category that you want to recognize. The accuracy of our model is directly proportional to the number of images in the set.
2. We need to make sure we have more relevant images in the image set. For example, if we have taken an image set with a single color background, say all the objects in the images have a white background and are shot indoors and users are trying to recognize objects with distracting backgrounds (colorful backgrounds shot outdoors), this won't result in better accuracy.

3. Choose images with a variety of backgrounds. For example, if we are picking images with only two background colors, then your prediction will have a preference toward those two colors rather than the object in the image.
4. Try to split bigger categories into smaller divisions. For example, instead of *animal*, we might use *cat, dog,* and *tiger*.
5. Make sure that we pick all the input images that have the objects that we are trying to recognize. For example, if we have a dog-recognizing app, we would not use cars, buildings, or mountains as input images. In that case, it is better to have a separate classifier for the unrecognizable images.
6. Ensure that we label images properly. For example, labeling a flower as *jasmine* might have the whole plant in the picture or a person behind it. The accuracy of our algorithm will differ when there are distracting objects in the input images.

We have taken a few food item images from Google images. These images have reusable permission, so always ensure that you have this when collecting images for your model. You can do this by searching any keyword from Google images and filtering the images based on *labeled for reuse* usage rights. We can find this option by clicking on **Tools** beneath the search bar.

We have collected a few reusable images from the internet and organized them under folders as follows:

```
$:cd ~/Chapter8/images
$:ls
dosa
idly
biriyani
burger
pizza
```

We keep around 100 images of each food item under the corresponding folder. Once our images are ready, we can run the training. These folder names are important since we are going to label all the food items inside each folder with the folder name. For example, all the food items under the `pizza` folder will be tagged as `pizza`.

When the data collection is done, we can start the training process through transfer learning.

Retraining with own images

We will use the `retrain.py` script in your project directory. Download this script using `curl`:

```
mkdir ~/Chapter8/images
cd ~/Chapter8/images
curl -LO
https://github.com/tensorflow/hub/raw/master/examples/image_retraining/
        retrain.py
```

There are a few parameters that we pass to the training script which we need to look into before the training starts.

Training steps parameter

Once we have our dataset ready, we need to look into improving the results. We can do this by altering the number of steps in the learning process. The simplest way to do this is to try the following:

```
--how_many_training_steps = 4000
```

The rate of accuracy improvement slows down when the number of steps increases, and the accuracy will stop improving beyond a certain point. You can experiment with this and decide what works best for you.

Architecture

MobileNet is a smaller, low-power, low-latency model designed to meet the constraints of mobile devices. In our application, we have picked the following architecture from the MobileNet datasets, which has a better accuracy benchmark:

```
--architecture="mobilenet_1.0_224"
```

The power and latency of the network grows with the number of **Multiply-Accumulates (MACs)**, which measure the number of fused multiplication and addition operations:

Model	Million MACs	Million Parameters	Top-1 Accuracy	Top-5 Accuracy
MobileNet_v1_1.0_224	569	4.24	70.9	89.9
MobileNet_v1_1.0_192	418	4.24	70.0	89.2
MobileNet_v1_1.0_160	291	4.24	68.0	87.7
MobileNet_v1_1.0_128	186	4.24	65.2	85.8
MobileNet_v1_0.75_224	317	2.59	68.4	88.2
MobileNet_v1_0.75_192	233	2.59	67.2	87.3
MobileNet_v1_0.75_160	162	2.59	65.3	86.0
MobileNet_v1_0.75_128	104	2.59	62.1	83.9
MobileNet_v1_0.50_224	150	1.34	63.3	84.9
MobileNet_v1_0.50_192	110	1.34	61.7	83.6
MobileNet_v1_0.50_160	77	1.34	59.1	81.9
MobileNet_v1_0.50_128	49	1.34	56.3	79.4
MobileNet_v1_0.25_224	41	0.47	49.8	74.2
MobileNet_v1_0.25_192	34	0.47	47.7	72.3
MobileNet_v1_0.25_160	21	0.47	45.5	70.3
MobileNet_v1_0.25_128	14	0.47	41.5	66.3

You can download the models from the following link: `https://github.com/tensorflow/models/blob/master/research/slim/nets/mobilenet_v1.md`.

Distortions

We can improve the results by giving tough input images during training. Training images can be generated by cropping, brightening, and deforming the input images randomly. This will help in generating an effective training dataset. However, there is a disadvantage of enabling distortion here, since bottleneck caching is not useful. Consequently, the input images are not reused, increasing the training time period. There are multiple ways to enable distortion as shown here:

```
--random_crop
--random_scale
--random_brightness
```

This won't be useful in all cases. For example, it won't be helpful in a digit classifier system, since flipping and distorting the image won't make sense when it comes to producing a possible output.

Hyperparameters

We can try a few more parameters to check whether additional parameters help to improve results.

Specify them in the form given in the bullets. The hyperparameters are explained as follows:

- `--learning_rate`: This parameter controls the updates to the final layer while training. If this value is small, the training will take more time. This may not always help when it comes to improving accuracy.
- `--train_batch_size`: This parameter helps with controlling the number of images examined during training to estimate the final layer updates. Once the images are ready, the script splits them into three different sets. The largest set is used in training. This division is mainly useful for preventing the model from recognizing unnecessary patterns in the input images. If a model is trained using a certain background pattern only, it won't give a proper result when it faces images with new backgrounds because it remembers unnecessary information from the input images. This is known as **overfitting**.

- `--testing_percentage` **and** `--validation_percentage` **flags**: To avoid overfitting, we keep 80% of the data inside the main training set. Of this data, 10% is then used to run validation during the training process and the final 10% is used to test the model. We can adjust these controls using the following parameters:
    - `--validation_batch_size`: We can see that the accuracy of validation fluctuates between iterations. This can be reduced by setting up the following parameter.

If you are new to this, you can run default values without making any changes to these parameters. Let's jump into building our model. For this, we need the training image data.

Running the training script

With all the parameter-related details discussed, we can start the training now with the downloaded script:

```
python retrain.py \
  --bottleneck_dir=./ \
  --how_many_training_steps=4000 \
  --model_dir=./ \
  --output_graph=./food_graph.pb \
  --output_labels=food_labels.txt \
  --architecture="mobilenet_1.0_224" \
  --image_dir=/Users/karthikeyan/Documents/docs/book/Chapter8/images
```

Based on our processor's capability as well as the number of images we have, the script might take longer for training. For me, it took more than 10 hours for 50 different food categories containing 1,500 images each. Once the script is completed, we will get the TensorFlow model in the output.

Model conversion

Once we have our TensorFlow model ready, we will convert this into a Core ML model. As we have done conversion in the other chapters, to get the latest version of the converter, clone this repository and install it from the source as follows:

```
git clone https://github.com/tf-coreml/tf-coreml.git
cd tf-coreml
```

Alternatively, install it using `pip`:

```
pip install -U tfcoreml
```

From the following code, we loop through the `graphDef` to find the information, because to convert the TensorFlow model to the Core ML model, we need to know some information.

We will get the following list of details from the following code:

- **Input name**: Output of the placeholder `op`, which is (`input:0`).
- **Output name**: Output of the softmax `op` toward the end of the graph, which is (`final_result:0`).
- **Model shape**: We get model shape from TensorBoard to find its shape during the model creation or we can also use `tf.shape()` to find its shape. Our model shape is [1, 224, 224, 3]. We can now convert it to Core ML model (`.mlmodel`):

```
import tensorflow as tf
import tfcoreml
from coremltools.proto import FeatureTypes_pb2 as _FeatureTypes_pb2
import coremltools

tf_model_path = "./food_graph.pb"
with open(tf_model_path , 'rb') as f:
    serialized = f.read()
tf.reset_default_graph()
original_gdef = tf.GraphDef()
original_gdef.ParseFromString(serialized)

with tf.Graph().as_default() as g:
    tf.import_graph_def(original_gdef, name ='')
    ops = g.get_operations()
    N = len(ops)
    for i in [0,1,2,N-3,N-2,N-1]:
        print('\n\nop id {} : op type: "{}"'.format(str(i),
                ops[i].type))
        print('input(s):')
        for x in ops[i].inputs:
            print("name = {}, shape: {}, ".format(x.name,
                    x.get_shape()))
        print('\noutput(s):'),
        for x in ops[i].outputs:
            print("name = {}, shape: {},".format(x.name,
                    x.get_shape()))
```

Here is the code block that converts the `.pb` model into the `.mlmodel` file:

```
""" CONVERT TensorFlow TO CoreML model """
# Model Shape
input_tensor_shapes = {"input:0":[1,224,224,3]}
# Input Name
image_input_name = ['input:0']
# Output CoreML model path
coreml_model_file = './food_graph.mlmodel'
# Output name
output_tensor_names = ['final_result:0']
# Label file for classification
class_labels = 'retrained_labels.txt'

#Convert Process
coreml_model = tfcoreml.convert(
        tf_model_path=tf_model_path,
        mlmodel_path=coreml_model_file,
        input_name_shape_dict=input_tensor_shapes,
        output_feature_names=output_tensor_names,
        image_input_names = image_input_name,
        class_labels = class_labels)
```

Now we have our Core ML model ready.

Here is the source code of the Python script: `https://github.com/intrepidkarthi/MLmobileapps/tree/master/Chapter8/tf_to_coreml.py`.

Once you download `tf_to_coreml.py` file you need modify the inputs like `tf_model_path`, `input_name_shape_dict`, `image_input_names`, and so on. based on the details of retrained model `food_graph.pb`. After the modification are done execute the below command to get the `food_graph.mlmodel`.

If you want to improve the accuracy performance of the model, you may need to look into a few more parameters:

```
coreml_model = tfcoreml.convert(
        tf_model_path=tf_model_path,
        mlmodel_path=coreml_model_file,
        input_name_shape_dict=input_tensor_shapes,
        output_feature_names=output_tensor_names,
        image_input_names = image_input_name,
        class_labels = class_labels,
        red_bias = -1,
        green_bias = -1,
```

```
blue_bias = -1,
image_scale = 2.0/255.0)
```

These additional parameters on the image bias will help in improving accuracy. Now we can jump into building the application.

Building the iOS application

We will create a new iOS application and import the ML model into it:

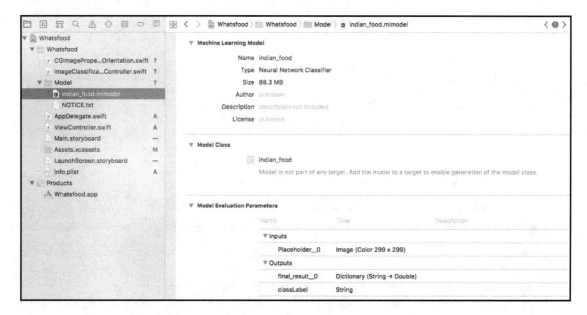

Once you select the `.mlmodel` file you will see the details about it and the important ones are ML model **Type**, **Inputs**, and **Outputs**. The **Inputs** type should be **image** because our input is going to be images of food item.

Once we have imported the model, we have to load the model into memory:

```
do {
/*
Use the Swift class `MobileNet` Core ML generates from the model.
To use a different Core ML classifier model, add it to the project
and replace `MobileNet` with that model's generated Swift class.
*/
let model = try VNCoreMLModel(for: food_graph().model)

let request = VNCoreMLRequest(model: model, completionHandler: { [weak
```

```
                    self] request, error in
          self?.processClassifications(for: request, error: error)
})
request.imageCropAndScaleOption = .centerCrop
return request
} catch {
fatalError("Failed to load Vision ML model: \(error)")
}
```

We will create a simple **User Interface** (**UI**) for the image classification through a storyboard:

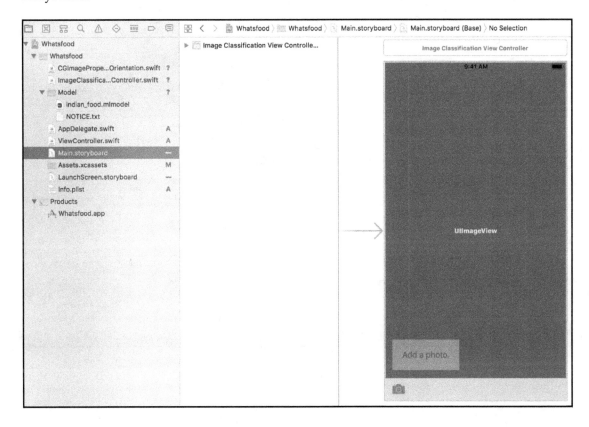

The UI is very simple where we will pick an image or snap a photo to identify the food classification. We will create the interface to satisfy the need. We will have to pick an image for our model to recognize and we will have two options to choose from, one is from camera-roll and other by clicking a picture of the food. We added a toolbar on the bottom of the screen and added a toolbar-item of camera type on top of it.

Toolbar item have an inbuilt type of camera so, you won't have to get a camera icon. We will have to show image of food item, so we will add an image view and then the constraints for it's position in the screen. We will add a button as shown in the preceding image with UI position constraints:

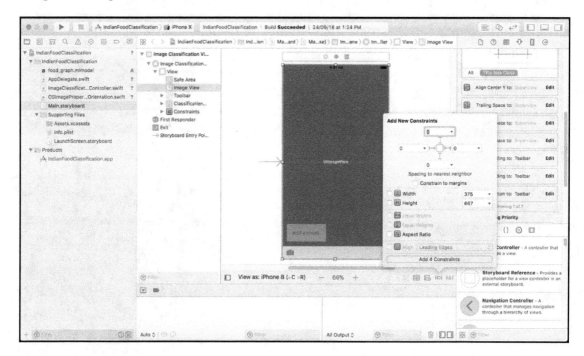

Select the view and add constraints on storyboard. After this we need to connect the view to the classes so that we can access it in run time. Connect the controls by dragging and dropping to the `ImageClassificationViewController.swift` class:

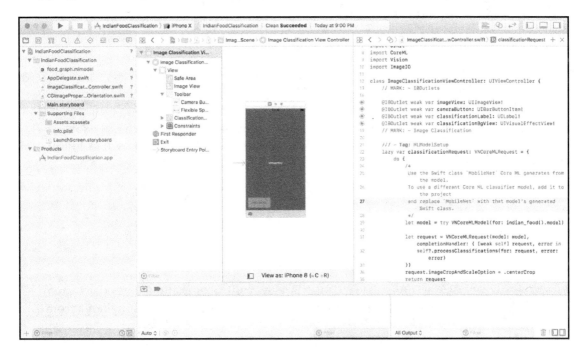

We will then add controls to take a picture from the camera and feed the input. The following method add controls launch a camera or a photo picker from the photo gallery. We will show the camera option only if the camera is available. We will add three actions on the photo picker to take photo, to pick image from gallery and to cancel the action popup:

```
@IBAction func takePicture() {
guard UIImagePickerController.isSourceTypeAvailable(.camera) else {
// Show options for the source picker only if the camera is available.
presentPhotoPicker(sourceType: .photoLibrary)
return
}

    let photoSourcePicker = UIAlertController()
    let takePhoto = UIAlertAction(title: "Take Photo", style:
                        .default) { [unowned self] _ in
        self.presentPhotoPicker(sourceType: .camera)
}

    let choosePhoto = UIAlertAction(title: "Choose Photo", style:
```

```
                                          .default) { [unowned self] _ in
        self.presentPhotoPicker(sourceType: .photoLibrary)
    }

    //Adding actions on the photo picker control
    photoSourcePicker.addAction(takePhoto)
    photoSourcePicker.addAction(choosePhoto)
    photoSourcePicker.addAction(UIAlertAction(title: "Cancel",
                                style:.cancel, handler: nil))

    present(photoSourcePicker, animated: true)
}
```

Now we will add a control that makes it possible to choose an image from the photo gallery. The control is passed on to `UIImagePickerController()` as shown as follows in the code block:

```
func presentPhotoPicker(sourceType: UIImagePickerControllerSourceType) {
    let picker = UIImagePickerController()
    picker.delegate = self
    picker.sourceType = sourceType
    present(picker, animated: true)
}
```

 `UIImagePickerController`: A view controller that manages the system interfaces for taking pictures, recording movies, and choosing items from the user's media library.

With the image-picker controls, we will add a view controller to call the image classification method. The following code shows how the image picker selection is handled. The code expects `imagePickerController(:didFinishPickingMediaWithInfo:)` to supply the input image:

```
extension ImageClassificationViewController:
UIImagePickerControllerDelegate, UINavigationControllerDelegate {
// Handling Image Picker Selection

func imagePickerController(_ picker: UIImagePickerController,
didFinishPickingMediaWithInfo info: [String: Any]) {
    picker.dismiss(animated: true)

    // We always expect
`imagePickerController(:didFinishPickingMediaWithInfo:)` to supply the
 original image.
    let image = info[UIImagePickerControllerOriginalImage] as! UIImage
    imageView.image = image
    updateClassifications(for: image)
```

```
    }
}
```

UIImagePickerControllerOriginalImage: Specifies the original,
uncropped image selected by the user.

From the controller, the classification method is called. Inside the method, image-processing handlers are added. The classificationRequest instances completion handler `processClassifications(_:error:)` catches errors specific to processing that request:

```
///Perform image classification requests
func updateClassifications(for image: UIImage) {
    classificationLabel.text = "Classifying..."
    classificationBgView.isHidden = false
    let orientation =
            CGImagePropertyOrientation(image.imageOrientation)
    guard let ciImage = CIImage(image: image) else {
        fatalError("Unable to create \(CIImage.self) from \(image).")
    }

    DispatchQueue.global(qos: .userInitiated).async {
    let handler = VNImageRequestHandler(ciImage: ciImage, orientation:
                                        orientation)
    do {
        try handler.perform([self.classificationRequest])
        } catch {
        print("Failed to perform classification.\n\
(error.localizedDescription)")
        }
    }
}
```

Once we receive the results from the model, we will update it back at the UI:

```
/// Updates the UI with the results of the classification.
/// - Tag: ProcessClassifications
func processClassifications(for request: VNRequest, error: Error?)        {
    DispatchQueue.main.async {
        guard let results = request.results else {
            self.classificationLabel.text = "Unable to classify image.\n\
                                        (error!.localizedDescription)"
            return
        }
// The `results` will always be `VNClassificationObservation`s, as
    specified by the Core ML model in this project.
        let classifications = results as! [VNClassificationObservation]

        if classifications.isEmpty {
            self.classificationLabel.text = "Nothing recognized."
        }
        else {
        // Display top classifications ranked by confidence in the UI.
        let topClassifications = classifications.prefix(2)
        let descriptions = topClassifications.map { classification in
        // Formats the classification for display; e.g. "(0.37) cliff,
            drop, drop-off".
        return String(format: " (%.2f) %@", classification.confidence,
                    classification.identifier)
        }
        self.classificationLabel.text = "Classification:\n" +
                descriptions.joined(separator: "\n")
    }
}
}
```

Here is a sample screenshot of our results:

Here is one sample image of our early model with improper datasets. Although we had 1,000+ photographs for each category of food, there was a few that had multiple dishes in them, as shown in the following screenshot graph. Our selection of inputs were bad as it contains a lot of noise surrounding the main food as there are multiple food items in a single image. This confused the algorithm, making it hard to get the desired results. Please try to avoid these kinds of issues when picking your dataset:

The preceding screenshot is another example with two detectable items in the same image where you can see the classifier values. You can see that both lollipops and idli vada are tagged here.

Summary

At this point, you should be able to build your own TensorFlow model as well as converting that into a Core ML model to be used in an iOS application. The same TensorFlow model can be converted into a TensorFlow Lite model to be used in an Android application. You can take up that task and experiment with the results there. With that, we will now move on to the next chapter.

In the next chapter, we will see how can you move ahead using the knowledge acquired from this book and how you can you build your own application.

What's Next?

9

Mobile phones have become the default consumption medium for most of the digital products that are being produced today. As data consumption increases, we have to get results to the user as soon as possible. For example, when you scroll your Facebook feed a lot of contents are loaded which you like from your friends and based on your interests. Since the time that user spend is very limited, there are a lot of algorithms run on the server side as well as client side to load and organize the content based on what your prefer on your Facebook feed. If there is a possibility to run all the algorithms on the local itself, we don't need to be dependent on the Internet to load the content faster.

This is only possible by performing the processing on the client's device itself, instead of processing in the cloud. As the processing capability of mobile devices increases, we will be encouraged to run all **machine learning (ML)** models on the mobile device itself. There are a lot of services that are already being processed on the client's device, such as identifying a face from a photo (such as Apple's Face ID feature), which uses ML on the local device.

While multiple topics are trending (such as **Artificial Intelligence (AI)**, **Augmented Reality (AR)**, **Virtual Reality (VR)**, blockchain, and ML), ML is growing faster than others, with proper use cases across all sectors. ML algorithms are being applied to images, text, audio, and video, in order to get the output that we desire.

If you are a beginner, there are multiple ways to start your work, by utilizing all of the free and open source frameworks that are being built. If you are worried about building a model yourself, you can start with ML Kit from Firebase and Google. Alternatively, you can build your own model by using TensorFlow, and convert that model to a TensorFlow Lite model (for Android) and a Core ML model (for iOS).

In this chapter, we will cover the following topics:

- A brief overview of the projects undertaken so far
- Popular ML-based cloud services
- Where to start when you build your first ML-based mobile app

What you have learned so far

In this book, we have covered seven mobile applications, using everyday, real-time use cases. In Chapter 1, *Mobile Landscapes in Machine Learning*, we covered the basics of ML-based applications, as well as the basics of building a model yourself. In Chapter 2, *CNN Based Age and Gender Identification Using Core ML*, you learned how to predict the age and gender of a person from an image or camera by using Core ML. In Chapter 3, *Applying Neural Style Transfer on Photos*, we applied a neural artistic-style transfer algorithm that is widely in use by image editing applications. This was done in the same way for both Android and iOS applications.

In Chapter 4, *Deep Diving into the ML Kit with Firebase*, we explored how to use the Firebase mobile SDK for face recognition, text prediction, and landmark prediction. If you are a beginner, you can start by utilizing the SDK on either Android or the iOS platform, without worrying about how to develop the model or how to generate data for it. In Chapter 5, *A Snapchat-like AR Filter on Android*, we looked at how to use another trending use case of ML, in AR. We built a real-time filter (similar to Snapchat) on the Android platform.

In Chapter 6, *Handwritten Digit Classifier Using Adversarial Learning*, you learned how to build a digit classifier with free handwriting, in real time. If the same model is implemented on an alphabet classifier, it will have a lot of use cases. In Chapter 7, *Face-Swapping with Your Friends Using OpenCV*, we looked at creating a popular online application that allows users to swap their faces with celebrities' faces. We did that using the dlib-ML toolkit and the OpenCV library. In Chapter 8, *Food Classification Using Transfer Learning*, we built our own model for implementing food classifiers, with the images sourced on our own.

Where to start when developing an ML application

To begin your ML journey, you can use one of the existing cloud based services on ML. **Machine learning as a Service (MLaaS)** is widely used across all contemporary business sectors. Data is becoming cheaper, and data volume is growing exponentially. As a result, devices' processing power is increasing at a much quicker rate. This trend has made way for multiple cloud-based services, such as **Software as a service (SaaS)**, **Platform as a service (PaaS)**, and **Infrastructure as a service (IaaS)**, now joined by MLaaS.

Even though we can run an ML model on our mobile device, it is still greatly limited to running most ML models on a local device due to limitation on memory and CPU/GPU. In this case, a cloud service comes in handy.

To start with ML in the cloud, there are multiple services available, such as facial recognition, optical character recognition, image recognition, landmark recognition, data visualization, **natural language processing** (**NLP**), and so on. All of these options are supported by deep neural networks, **Convolutional Neural Networks** (**CNNs**), probabilistic models, and other options. Most cloud providers are running a business model that has some free limits for a developer to explore, before deciding which is the best fit to develop their application. The following sections will explain the four major services that are available now, and are popular among developers and enterprises. As a beginner, you can explore the functionality under each provider and pick the one that suits your application.

IBM Watson services

IBM Watson provides deep learning as a service through a variety of products. There is a bot service over text, called **AI assistant**, which supports mobile platforms and chat services, and there is another service, called **Watson Studio**. This is helpful for building and analyzing the model. IBM Watson also has another, separate API service, which processes text, vision, and speech.

There is a sample application available for developing a vision application using Core ML. This can be found at `https://github.com/watson-developer-cloud/visual-recognition-coreml`.

Microsoft Azure Cognitive Services

Microsoft provides out-of-the-box Cognitive Services in five categories, as follows:

- **Vision APIs**: Image processing algorithms to smartly identify, caption, and moderate your pictures.
- **Speech APIs**: Through these, we can convert spoken audio to text, use voices for verification, or add speaker recognition to an application.
- **Knowledge APIs**: These help to map complex information and data, in order to solve tasks such as intelligent recommendations and semantic searches.
- **Search APIs**: These provide Bing Web Search APIs to apps and harness the ability to comb billions of web pages, images, videos, and news, with a single API call.
- **Language APIs**: These allow your apps to process natural language with pre-built scripts, evaluate sentiments, and learn how to recognize what users want.

There are multiple sample applications for the preceding APIs. These can be found at `https://azure.microsoft.com/en-in/resources/samples/?sort=0`.

Amazon ML

Amazon AWS has multiple offerings for ML-based services. All of these services are tightly coupled, in order to work efficiently in the AWS cloud. A few of the services are as follows:

- **Vision services**: AWS has Amazon Recognition, which is a deep learning-based service that is designed to process image and video. We can integrate the service on mobile devices, as well.
- **Chat services**: Amazon Lex helps to build chatbots. This industry is still growing, with more and more data coming in; the service will become more intelligent, allowing it to answer queries even better.
- **Language services**: Examples of these include Amazon Comprehend, which helps to discover insights and relationships in text; Amazon Translate, which helps with the fluent translation of text; Amazon Transcribe, which helps with automatic speech recognition; and Amazon Polly, which helps to turn natural-sounding text into speech.

 You can see a few sample applications at `https://github.com/aws-samples/machine-learning-samples`.

Google Cloud ML

If you want to run your model in the cloud, the Google Cloud ML Engine offers the power and flexibility of TensorFlow, scikit-learn, and XGBoost in the cloud. If this is not suitable, you can pick the API services that best fit your scenario.

In Google Cloud ML, multiple APIs are available. These are classified into four major categories, as follows:

- **SIGHT**: The Cloud Vision API helps with image recognition and classification; the Cloud Video Intelligence API helps with scene-level video annotation; and AutoML Vision helps with custom image classification models.

- **CONVERSATION**: Dialogflow Enterprise Edition helps to build conversational interfaces; the Cloud Text-to-Speech API converts text to speech; and the Cloud Speech-to-Text API converts speech to text.
- **LANGUAGE**: The Cloud Translation API is used in language detection and translation; the Cloud Natural Language API is used in text parsing and analysis; AutoML Translation is used in custom domain-specific translation; and AutoML Natural Language helps in building custom text classification models.
- **KNOWLEDGE**: The Cloud Inference API helps to derive insights from time-series datasets.

You can find a few Google Vision APIs at `https://github.com/GoogleCloudPlatform/cloud-vision`.

There are also other services that are popular with developers, including `api.ai` and `wit.ai`.

Building your own model

With the knowledge that you gained from this book, you can start to develop your own model that runs on a mobile phone. You will need to identify the problem statement first. There are many use cases where you will not need an ML model; we can't unnecessarily force ML into everything. Consequently, you need to follow a step-by-step approach before you build your own model:

1. Identify the problem.
2. Plan the effectiveness of your model; decide whether the data could be useful in predicting output for future, similar cases. For example, collecting the purchase history for people of a similar age, gender, and location would be helpful in predicting a new customer's purchase preferences. However, the data wouldn't be helpful in predicting the height of a new customer, if that is the data that you are looking for.
3. Develop a simple model; this can be based on SQL. It will be useful for reducing the effort when building actual models.
4. Validate the data and throw the unnecessary data out.
5. Build the actual model.

As data is growing exponentially on various parameters(data from multiple sensors) on the local devices (as well as with cloud providers), we can build better use cases with more and more personalized content. There are many applications that are already using ML.

Limitations of building your own model

While ML is getting popular, it is not yet feasible to running ML models on mobile platforms to reach the masses. When you are building your own model for mobile apps, there are some limitations, as well. While it is possible to make predictions on a local device without a cloud service, it is not advisable to build an evolving model that makes predictions based on your current actions and accumulates data, evolving on the local device itself. As of right now, we can run pre-built models and get inferences out of them on mobile devices, due to the constraints on memory and the processing power of the mobile devices. Once we have better processors on a mobile device, we can train and improve the model on the local device.

There are a lot of use cases related to this. Apple's Face ID is one such example, running a model on a local device that requires computations from a CPU or GPU. When the device's capability increases in the future, it will be possible to build a completely new model on the device itself.

Accuracy is another reason why people refrain from developing models on their mobile devices. Since we are currently unable to run heavy operations on our mobile devices, the accuracy, as compared to a cloud-based service, seems bleak. The reason being the limitation on both memory and computational capability. You could run the models that are available for mobile devices in the TensorFlow and Core ML libraries.

 The Tensorflow Lite models can be found at `https://www.tensorflow.org/lite/models`, and the Core ML models can be found at `https://github.com/likedan/Awesome-CoreML-Models`.

Personalized user experience

A personalized **user experience** (UX) will be the basic use case for any mobile based consumer business, to provide a more curated and personalized experience for the users of their mobile applications. This can be done by analyzing data points such as the following:

- Who is your customer?
- Where do they come from?
- What are their interests?

- What do they say about you?
- Where did they find you?
- Do they have any pain points?
- Can they afford your products?
- Do they have a history of purchases or searches?

For example, consider a customer of a retail company or a restaurant; if we have answers to the preceding questions, we have rich data about the customers, from which we can build data models that will provide more personalized experiences (with the help of ML). We can analyze and identify similar customers, to provide a better UX for all of the users, as well as targeting the right future customers.

Better search results

Providing the better search result is one of the major use cases, especially on a mobile application, to provide more contextual results, rather than text-based results. This will help to improve the businesses' customer bases. ML algorithms should learn from user searches and optimize the results. Even spelling corrections can be done intuitively. Moreover, collecting users' behavioral data (concerning how they use your app) will be helpful in providing the best search results, so that you can rank the results in a way that is more personalized to the user.

Targeting the right user

Most apps capture the users' age and gender data when they install the application for the first time. This will help you to understand the common user group of your application. You will also have user data about their usage and frequency of use, as well as location data, if that is permitted from the user's end. This will be helpful in predicting future customer targets. For example, you will be able to see if your user audience is coming from the age group of 18-25 and is predominantly female. In that case, you could devise a strategy to pull more male users, or just stick to targeting female users only. The algorithm should be able to predict and analyze all of this data, which will be helpful in marketing and increasing your user base.

There are a lot of niche use cases where Machine Learning based mobile apps can be of great help. Some of them are as follows:

- Automatic product tagging
- Time estimations like in pedometer, uber, lyft
- Health-based recommendations
- Shipping cost estimations
- Supply chain predictions
- Money management
- Logistics optimization
- Increasing productivity

Summary

With all of the basic ideas that you have gained from this book, you can start to build your own application with ML capabilities. Furthermore, with all of the new ways to interact with devices such as Amazon Alexa, Google Home, or the Facebook portal, you will find more and more use cases to build ML applications. Ultimately, we are moving toward a world with more and more connected devices, which brings the connections and communications closer to us which leads us to make more and more better experiences with ML.

Further reading

- There are a lot of ML courses available online. If you are beginner, you can start with the Coursera tutorial on *Machine Learning* by Andrew Ng, which can be found at https://www.coursera.org/learn/machine-learning.
- A *Machine Learning Crash Course* from Google can be found at https://developers.google.com/machine-learning/crash-course/.
- One of the best (and most enlightening) ML-based blog series, by Adam Geitgey, can be found at https://medium.com/@ageitgey/machine-learning-is-fun-80ea3ec3c471.
- You can kick-start your skills in TensorFlow at https://codelabs.developers.google.com/codelabs/tensorflow-for-poets/; a more thorough look can be found at https://petewarden.com/2016/09/27/tensorflow-for-mobile-poets/.

Other Books You May Enjoy

If you enjoyed this book, you may be interested in these other books by Packt:

Intelligent Mobile Projects with TensorFlow
Jeff Tang

ISBN: 9781788834544

- Classify images with transfer learning
- Detect objects and their locations
- Transform pictures with amazing art styles
- Understand simple speech commands
- Describe images in natural language
- Recognize drawing with Convolutional Neural Network and Long Short-Term Memory
- Predict stock price with Recurrent Neural Network in TensorFlow and Keras
- Generate and enhance images with generative adversarial networks
- Build AlphaZero-like mobile game app in TensorFlow and Keras
- Use TensorFlow Lite and Core ML on mobile
- Develop TensorFlow apps on Raspberry Pi that can move, see, listen, speak, and learn

Machine Learning with Swift

Alexander Sosnovshchenko

ISBN: 9781787121515

- Learn rapid model prototyping with Python and Swift
- Deploy pre-trained models to iOS using Core ML
- Find hidden patterns in the data using unsupervised learning
- Get a deeper understanding of the clustering techniques
- Learn modern compact architectures of neural networks for iOS devices
- Train neural networks for image processing and natural language processing

Leave a review - let other readers know what you think

Please share your thoughts on this book with others by leaving a review on the site that you bought it from. If you purchased the book from Amazon, please leave us an honest review on this book's Amazon page. This is vital so that other potential readers can see and use your unbiased opinion to make purchasing decisions, we can understand what our customers think about our products, and our authors can see your feedback on the title that they have worked with Packt to create. It will only take a few minutes of your time, but is valuable to other potential customers, our authors, and Packt. Thank you!

Index